Econometric Wage and Price Models

Econometric Wage and Price Models

Assessing the Impact of the Economic Stabilization Program

A. Bradley Askin
University of California, Irvine

John Kraft
University of Florida

Lexington Books
D.C. Heath and Company
Lexington, Massachusetts
Toronto   London

Library of Congress Cataloging in Publication Data

Askin, A   Bradley.
  Econometric wage and price models.

  Includes bibliographical references.
  1. Wage-price policy–United States–Mathematical models. I. Kraft, John, joint author. II. Title.
HC110.W24A83   331.2'1'01   73-11658
ISBN 0-669-85506-5

Published simultaneously in Canada.

Printed in the United States of America.

International Standard Book Number: 0-669-85506-5

Library of Congress Catalog Card Number: 73-11658

Contents

List of Figures

List of Tables

Preface

In the Spring of 1972, one of us (Askin) suggested to Robert Lanzillotti, then a member of the Price Commission, that econometric studies be undertaken within the Price Commission for the purposes of forecasting the economy, ascertaining the impact Phase II was having, and evaluating potential policy changes in the Economic Stabilization Program. At the subsequent request of the Price Commission, that coauthor initiated an econometric study of wage and price models as a consultant in the Division of Price Analysis, which was a branch of the Price Commission's Office of Price Policy. Shortly thereafter the other coauthor (Kraft) also joined this project as a consultant.

The wage and price analyses undertaken as part of this econometric project are described in *Report on Econometric Wage and Price Models*, an unpublished Price Commission study.[1] While all the material in this book has been updated and revised or conceived since the completion of the work done for the Price Commission, that work and the report on it constitute an important input without which the present book would not have been written. We wish to acknowledge the support the Price Commission provided for that earlier, preliminary report. Ahmad Al-Sammarrie and Blaine Roberts, as the head and assistant head of the Division of Price Analysis, assigned us research assistants and obtained computer time, kept pressures for premature outputs to a minimum, and commented on technical aspects of the project. Robert Lakoski and Raymond Yacouby served ably as research assistants at various stages of the project. Rachel Kronstadt helped in collecting and coding much of the data.

For all the revisions and further work undertaken since the completion of the Price Commission study, we assume all responsibility for errors. Gini Nordyke and Mrs. Susi LaVasseur typed the manuscript. Ms. Nordyke also drew many of the figures used throughout the book.

A. Bradley Askin
John Kraft

1

Introduction

For the last several years, during which the new found macroeconomic policies of the sixties have been impotent in holding down wages and prices, and the conventional notion of a tradeoff between unemployment and inflation has become inoperative, the United States has witnessed the worst combination of high unemployment and rapid inflation in its postwar history. What few Americans realize is that inflation and unemployment problems are not the exclusive property of this country. Over the last decade the chief economic concern for most industrial nations has been an explosion of wages and prices. Table 1-1 shows that other countries currently face even more severe problems of this kind than does the United States.

A number of countries—including, for example, Italy, West Germany, Japan, Sweden, Great Britain, and France—have experimented with incomes policies designed to meet their inflation difficulties. On August 15, 1971, the U.S. joined the incomes policy derby by announcing a comprehensive 90-day freeze on wages and prices, to be followed for as long as necessary by more flexible Phases II and III controls programs. While the freeze represented a dramatic turn in U.S. policy, in that it marked the first time mandatory controls had ever been imposed in peacetime, it cannot be viewed so dramatically in the context of the policies adopted by other nations.

Table 1-1
Annual Percentage Rates of Inflation in Consumer Prices for Selected Countries

Country	1955-1972	1966-1972	1972
United States	2.58	4.13	3.36
Canada	2.59	3.98	4.99
West Germany	2.86	3.64	6.64
Italy	3.62	3.90	7.44
United Kingdom	4.17	5.73	8.04
Japan	4.57	5.61	6.05
France	4.68	5.00	6.87

Source: U.S. Department of Commerce, Bureau of Census, *Business Conditions Digest* for all countries except the U.S.; U.S. Department of Labor, Bureau of Labor Statistics, Consumer Price Index for the U.S.

Note: Annual average rates of inflation were computed from nonseasonally adjusted monthly consumer price indexes.

1

Econometric Wage and Price Models

Evaluating the impact of any incomes policy is a complex and difficult undertaking, for it requires that the behavior of wages and prices under the program be compared with the hypothetical behavior which would have occurred in the absence of the program. One way to estimate what this hypothetical behavior would have been is to fit an econometric model of wages and prices to the precontrol period, simulate this model for the controls period to determine what would have happened without an incomes policy, and then compare this simulated behavior of wages and prices with their actual behavior while controls were in effect. The problem is in choosing the proper econometric model of wages and prices.

Briefly stated, there are several reasons why the adoption of an econometric approach is beneficial. First, developing the equations of an econometric model requires a systematic specification of the proposed relationships among economic variables. This specification aids in conceptualizing alternative hypotheses and drawing attention to areas of disagreement. Second, empirically applying alternative models allows a comparison of their properties and the explanatory power of the hypotheses underlying them. It permits both replication with other data sets to test for generality and transfers of variables among models to study how their impacts depend on the context in which they are used. Third, once a model has been estimated, simulating it provides a means of preparing forecasts and evaluating policy alternatives. By making minor, and major, changes in the values assigned to individual variables and observing whether simulated outcomes change significantly, the sensitive variables which have important consequences for forecasts and policy proposals can be distinguished from other variables.

Over the years an overwhelming number of wage and price studies have appeared which attempt to explain the behavior of wages and prices for both the United States and other nations.[1] Based on a wide variety of competing theories and models, these efforts have taken on many forms. Some have focused on the determination of wages, others on the explanation of prices, and still others on both wages and prices. A variety of variables have been used to explain wages and prices.

Econometric studies of wage determination have been particularly concerned with identifying and distinguishing the relative importance of alternative forces theorized to affect wages. The most widely tested function postulates a relationship between the percentage change in money wage rates and conditions in the labor market, with the price of labor varying with the degree of excess demand in the labor market. Phillips, who authored the first widely known study of this type, used the unemployment rate, the change in it, and the percentage change in prices in his wage equation.[2]

Criticisms of the unemployment rate as an appropriate measure of excess demand have precipitated the development of a number of other measures designed to replace or supplement it as a proxy for labor market tightness. For instance, Vroman, Simler and Tella, and Gordon have all used variations of the labor reserve theme to explain changes in wage rates.[3] The labor reserve concept attempts to get a truer picture of how tight the labor market is, by identifying the number of individuals not counted as being unemployed because they have dropped out of the labor force. Other alternatives to the unemployment rate have been utilized by MacRae *et al.*, Perry, and Gordon.[4] MacRae *et al.* used the ratio of job vacancies to unemployment to define a measure of net labor market tightness. Perry attempted to distinguish between the unemployment of primary and secondary workers with a weighted unemployment variable, and also defined an unemployment dispersion variable on the grounds that different classes of labor form imperfect substitutes. Gordon used several of these variables in tandem rather than any one of them as a single measure of excess demand.

As evidence has accumulated that labor market conditions provide an incomplete explanation of wage behavior, increasing attention has been paid to the hypothesis that price expectations affect wages significantly. This expectations impact, usually approximated by a distributed lag of past rates of price change, has been tested in two versions.[5] The simpler version postulates a linear relationship between price expectations and wage changes. The more sophisticated version proposes an inflationary expectations threshold, below which the impact on wages is slight and above which it is substantial. This threshold has been explained both on the basis of partial worker money illusion and on the basis of correlation among union bargaining power, the business cycle and the pace of inflation. Both forms of the expectations approach have been criticized because of the double causation implied between wages and prices and the inability to separate out the source of the causality.[6]

A number of studies have introduced productivity into the wage equation on the rationale that workers argue for and obtain higher wages to the extent that their increased effectiveness results in a lowering of unit labor costs. Kuh has taken this approach to its logical extreme, based on classical arguments that productivity is the major determinant of real wages.[7] Still others have stressed profits as a determining factor in the wage equation. Perry, for example, has argued that higher profits made firms more susceptible to meeting worker demands for higher wages as a means of sharing in the firms' success, and that unions become more adamant in making these demands.[8] Kuh has challenged the use of profits with the claim that they show up significantly in wage equations only as a proxy for productivity, owing to the boost productivity increases give to profits.

Most research on the price side has been directed towards public policy issues relating to monopoly. Accordingly, it has been primarily concerned with ascertaining whether prices are competitively determined by supply and demand

forces in the market or administratively set by firms following target rate of
return or full cost pricing rules, not with identifying which particular influences
best explain prices. The majority of studies have concluded that prices are at
least partly administered as opposed to perfectly competitive.[9]

Unit labor costs have generally been used as the main driving force behind
prices in the long run. Gordon combined wages and productivity into the same
unit labor cost variable, while Eckstein and Brinner allowed them to have
separate effects.[10] Some studies have used standard unit labor costs, while
others have used actual ones. In some studies limited to the manufacturing
sector, such as those by Moffat, and Siebert and Zaidi, raw material costs have
also been allowed to play a secondary long run role in determining prices.[11]
Where unit labor costs have appeared as the only long run factor, prices have
almost always been expected to have an elasticity of one with respect to labor
costs; where raw materials prices and other long run variables have also appeared,
unit labor costs have been assigned a smaller impact.

Owing to the difficulty of measuring capital costs, they have not been
included among the variables explaining prices. Instead, they have been left as an
unexplained residual, subsumed in various measures of product market excess
demand conditions, and used to show how changes in product market conditions
affect the markup of prices over costs in the short run. A wide variety of
product market variables have been used: unfilled orders, net new orders,
capacity utilization rates, inventory to sales ratios, and the like. Siebert and
Zaidi used both the capacity utilization rate and an unfilled orders to sales ratio
variable in attempting to separate those demand factors which keep costs and
prices down from those that push them up.[12]

Based on the empirical ability of the many theories to explain wages and
prices, it appears that a number of the competing wage and price functions can
be characterized as equally capable. Choosing among the conflicting views of the
inflation process presented in these models has proven a confounding problem.
Different studies have used different data sources, different time periods, and
even different definitions of what appear to be nominally identical variables in
analyzing wages and prices in different sectors of the economy. Both our reading
of the literature and our own empirical analyses suggest that the alternative
equations are neither unique nor complete and that formulating wage and price
models is more context specific than universally precise. Owing to the
uniqueness of the postwar inflation episodes, there have simply not been enough
data on repetitions of similar market conditions with which to distinguish among
alternative explanations of wage and price behavior.[13]

Scope of the Book

In this book we replicate three recently published studies of wage and price behavior with a common set of data for the private nonfarm economy. Our purpose is twofold. First, we want to ascertain whether the apparent differences among the three studies truly stem from their specifications or merely reflect their different data bases. Our concern is not in choosing among specific hypotheses regarding wages and prices per se, but in analyzing the inflation process as a whole. Second, and more important, we want to answer certain questions concerning the U.S. venture into a mandatory incomes policy program with the 90–day wage-price freeze and Phase II. Among the questions to be answered are: (1) was the Economic Stabilization Program necessary, or had inflation already peaked; (2) if the controls were necessary, was the program successful in controlling wages and prices; (3) how did the program influence the equilibrium tradeoff between inflation and unemployment?

We will not be concerned with analyzing either the individual regulations of the Price Commission and the Pay Board or the relative benefits and costs of the Economic Stabilization Program. Analyses of the controls program regulations are available elsewhere, while undertaking a benefit-cost study would require another book in itself.[14]

Chapters 2, 3, and 4 are concerned with defining and estimating the three models we use. Each of the models is treated in a separate chapter where we present the wage and price equation for that model; estimate these equations over what we have selected as our historical period; simulate the estimated model over the historical period; and solve for the long run Phillips curve implied by the model.

Chapter 5 compares the performances of the three models in tracking inflation during the historical period. The explanatory power of the estimated structural wage and price equations, the accuracy of the simulations over the historical period, and the long run Phillips curves are used as the criteria for this comparison.

The remainder of the book is concerned with an evaluation of the Economic Stabilization Program based on extensions of the three models. Chapter 6 presents detailed results on the simulation of the economy for the period of mandatory controls beginning in August, 1971, both with and without an incomes policy. It follows four steps. First, the models for the historical period are simulated over the period of the controls program as an indication of how wages and prices would have performed in an economy without controls. Second, a dummy variable proxy for the controls program is added to the equations of the historical models, and these controls versions of the equations are reestimated over an expanded period, including the wage and price controls program, to provide a measure of the direct impact of the program on wages and prices. Third, each of the reestimated controls models is simulated to determine the total impact which controls had in moderating inflation. Fourth, the long run Phillips curve for each controls model is derived and compared with its historical model counterpart to show how the Phillips curve shifted.

Chapter 7 undertakes two tasks. First, forecasts of the future performance of wages and prices are presented under varying assumptions about the unemployment rate and the impact of the controls program. These forecasts should assist the reader in making his own assessment of the controls' longer run impacts. Second, our main findings are summarized and their implications discussed.

Summary Comments on Methodology

In order to maximize the consistency of our analysis and ensure a proper comparison of the three models we employ, all of the models were applied with a common data base covering the identical historical period. The private, nonfarm economy was used as the frame of reference throughout. Unless stated to the contrary, all variables refer to it. Variables were constructed on a quarterly basis; except for one explanatory variable, one-quarter rates of change were used, although frequently in lagged form. In contrast to a number of studies, all rate variables referring either to a point in time or a change over time were expressed in decimal form as opposed to percentage form.

Choosing the private, nonfarm economy as the frame of reference excluded the government sector, where prices serve a different function and are determined by different forces than in the private economy, and the agriculture sector, where prices are subject to fluctuations caused by weather and international market phenomena distinct from those affecting U.S. prices in general. From the standpoint of assessing the impacts of the Economic Stabilization Program excluding these two sectors is salutory, for both were exempted from the controls regulations.

For our historical period we used the 66-quarter span of time from the first quarter of 1955 through the second quarter of 1971. We selected this period in order to maximize the number of observations available, while excluding the influences of the Korean Conflict and the controls program initiated with the August 15,1971, announcement of the 90-day wage and price freeze.

The use of ordinary least squares (OLS) regression techniques in a simultaneous system of equations, such as all our models use to explain wages and prices, violates the assumptions of least squares estimators and yields biased and inconsistent parameter estimates. Nevertheless, certain considerations led us to estimate OLS regressions, as opposed to using two stage least squares or another theoretically justified technique. First, the original versions of the models presented in Chapter 2,3, and 4 were estimated with OLS regressions, and we wanted to replicate these earlier versions as closely as possible. Second, previous wage and price studies using simultaneous equations techniques have found that the bias associated with relying on OLS techniques is quite small for wage and price equations.[15] Third, in the case of two of our models the utilization of simultaneous equations techniques would have required greatly complicating the analysis or changing the models.[a] While our third model could easily have been estimated with simultaneous equations techniques, we saw little reason for using them for just the one model without applying them to the other two models as well. Fourth, our simulations of the models provide for the feedback of wages and prices on one another, in what we considered adequate fashion, to detect any biases introduced by our reliance on OLS techniques, though not to eliminate them. Except in two instances, discussed in later chapters where they arise, we found such biases to be negligible.

---

[a]Many of the variables in the distributed lag adjustment model of Chapter 2 are introduced in Almon lags. Simultaneous equations bias could be eliminated from this model, only by taking the current values of such variables out of the lag structure and using simultaneous equations estimation procedures, or beginning the lags in the past, so as to render them entirely predetermined. Either approach, even if the former one were applied with coefficient restrictions placed on the relationship between current period and past period coefficients, would preclude replicating the freely determined lags of the original study. The imposed lag adjustment model of Chapter 3 introduces most of its variables in an imposed lag. Here, simultaneous equations techniques could be applied with coefficient restrictions that would retain the original imposed lag, but at significant cost in terms of complicating the estimation procedure.

2

A Distributed Lag Adjustment Model

The distributed lag adjustment (henceforth DLA) model described in this chapter, originally developed by Robert J. Gordon in an earlier study, differs from other models of the inflation process in several noteworthy respects.[1] First, a number of transformations are made in published data series generally employed in wage and price models in order to construct variables more appropiate from the standpoint of economic theory. Second, Almon distributed lags are used to capture the disequilibrium movements of wages and prices in response to changes in explanatory variables, Third, an unusually long six-year price expectations lag, corresponding to the distributed lags of similar length used elsewhere to explain interest rates, is imposed into the wage equation.[2]

In applying this DLA model, we have kept modifications of it from the original form used by Gordon to a minimum, in order to facilitate comparison of our results with his. Thus, his lag specifications have been retained, even though we found alternatives which worked marginally better for certain variables. All of the distributed lags are fourth degree Almon polynomial lags, estimated with lag coefficient restricted to zero for the period immediately preceding in time the far period in the lag.[a] We have made four minor changes in the model. While maintaining the long lag on price expectations, we have estimated it directly in the wage equation, as opposed to imposing the relative lag weights from a separately estimated interest rate equation. We think the directly estimated lag more appropriate, as well as computationally simpler.[b] In addition, we have estimated the wage equation with one-quarter rate of change observations, rather than with the overlapping two-quarter rate of change observations Gordon employed to minimize serial correlation difficulties. This modification does produce serially correlated residuals, but greatly facilitates comparisons among the three models we test. Finally, we have used the reciprocal of one variable rather than the variable itself and different data for another, as discussed below.

---

[a] According to Gordon, his lagged coefficients are not only restricted to zero in the most distant period, but also approach zero asymptotically. See [18, p. 147]. Our regression package did not have this latter capability. While we have kept the fourth degree polynomial form of his lag, we are skeptical about its theoretical justification in the present context. This point is crucial for the long price expectations lag, which performs better than a much shorter lag only when more than a second degree polynomial is allowed. See footnote j in this chapter.

[b] Contrary to Gordon's argument, we see no reason why consumer price expectations should necessarily be formed in the same manner as are interest rate expectations. Consequently, tying the price expectations lag structure to an interest rate expectations lag structure strikes us as inappropriate.

9

Specification of the DLA Model

The distributed lag adjustment model consists of two equations, one explaining standard unit labor costs and another explaining prices, which explicitly take into account the interactions between wages and prices in the inflation process. Complete definitions of all variables and descriptions of all data sources are provided in Appendixes A and B, respectively.

The Wage Equation

As briefly discussed in the introductory chapter, econometric studies of wage behavior have employed a myriad of theoretical models. The DLA wage equation can be categorized as eclectic, in that it includes variables designed to capture several of the factors that have been found important in previous empirical studies. The wage equation to be fitted is

$$\left(\frac{\dot{W}}{Q^*}\right)_t = a + b\,DU_t + c\,UD_t + d\,UH_t + e\,\dot{PCD}_{L,t}$$

$$+ f(P\dot{NFD} - \dot{PCD})_{L,t-1} + g\,T(\dot{E})_t + h\,T(\dot{F})_{L,t}. \qquad (2.1)$$

The t subscripts refer to quarter-year time periods; the L subscripts indicate the use of an Almon distributed lag on the variable, beginning in the referenced time period with the sum of the individual lag coefficients reported as the variable coefficient. Dots above variables indicate their use in rate of change form.

The dependent variable in this wage equation is not the rate of change in wages per se, but the one-quarter rate of change in standard unit labor costs. Standard unit labor costs are found by dividing a fixed weight index of gross wages, including fringe benefits and adjusted for interindustry employment shifts and manufacturing overtime, paid to production workers by the trend value of output per manhour. The variable is measured over the private, nonfarm economy.

The first three explanatory variables are intended to capture in combination the impact labor market conditions have on standard unit labor costs by affecting wages. DU_t is an index of unemployment dispersion. It measures the variation of unemployment rates weighted by wage rates and hours worked among sectors of the labor force delineated by age and sex. Weighting the sector unemployment rates treats labor as homogeneous within sectors, yet recognizes the different quantities and qualities of it among sectors. The hypothesis underlying the construction of DU_t is that labor force groups are imperfect substitutes for one another. This implies that an increase in unemployment dispersion tightens the labor market for a constant overall unemployment rate. Since this tightening of the labor market in turn increases the upward pressure on wages, an increase in unemployment dispersion should lead to a more rapid increase in standard unit labor costs. Consequently, b is expected to be positive.[c]

UD_t is a measure of disguised unemployment, equal to the quotient of the difference between the potential and actual labor forces divided by the actual labor force. Disguised unemployment is inversely related to labor force tightness for two interrelated reasons: the net entry of additional people into the labor force, when the labor market tightens, both reduces the gap between the potential and actual labor forces and causes the latter to grow. Inasmuch as labor market tightness causes wages and standard unit labor costs to rise faster, c is expected to be negative.

UH_t is the unemployment rate of hours, defined as 1.0 minus the ratio of actual to potential hours of work in the private, nonfarm economy. The unemployment rate of hours is inversely related to labor market tightness, because more individuals work, and they work longer hours on the average, when the labor market tightens. As with the coefficient on disguised unemployment, this inverse relationship between the unemployment rate of hours and labor market tightness should cause d to be negative.

$\dot{PCD}_t$ is the one-quarter rate of change in the GNP implicit price deflator for personal consumption expenditures. It is used in a distributed lag, denoted by the subscript L, as a measure of price expectations on the ground that workers form expectations about future inflation by extrapolating past inflation experience with respect to the prices they pay as consumers. Implicit in the particular lag structure used is the notion that workers form their expectations about inflation only partially on the basis of what has happened most recently, with complete adjustment requiring a lapse of six years as successive partial adjustments cumulate. Owing to the fact that the real wage increase associated with any given increase in their money wage varies inversely with the rate of change in the prices they pay as consumers, workers have an incentive to adjust their wage demands according to the extent of price inflation they expect. Moreover, the strength of this incentive changes as these expectations do, for the benefit to workers in real purchasing power terms of passing inflation on to their employers in the form of higher wages increases as the rate of inflation increases.

---

[c]Gordon justified the utilization of DU_t as an explanatory variable in the wage equation on the grounds that an increase in unemployment dispersion tightens the labor market for a given overall unemployment rate, because the relationship between unemployment and the rate of wage increase is convex to the origin. See [18, p. 109]. This places undue emphasis on the nonlinearity of the Phillips curve for the labor market as a whole and for sectors thereof. Our rationale for including DU_t in the wage equation does not depend on the shape, or even existence, of the Phillips curve in any way.

In "normal" times of little inflation a zero pass-through would inflict minor purchasing power losses on workers, while in periods of rapid inflation anything less than 100 percent pass-through could impose significant costs on them.[d] Reflecting the fact that the wage equation captures only the average impact price expectations have in boosting wages as an element of standard unit labor costs, e the sum of the coefficients on the distributed lag series of price expectation variables, is expected to be positive but less than unity.

$P\dot{N}FD_t$ is the one-quarter rate of change in the GNP implicit price deflator for the private, nonfarm deflator. Used to measure the rate of change in product prices, it corresponds in slightly modified form to the fixed weight price index Gordon used.[e] Therefore, $(P\dot{N}FD - P\dot{C}D)_{L, t-1}$ provides a distributed lag measure of the divergence between product prices in general and consumer prices in particular. This latter variable is used in the wage equation to capture the lagged labor demand effects price changes have on standard unit labor costs, as differentiated from the labor supply effects they have traceable to price expectations. $(P\dot{N}FD - P\dot{C}D)_{L, t-1}$ is used instead of a lag structure on just $P\dot{N}FD_t$ so as to minimize multicollinearity problems, and has its coefficient restricted to zero in the current period so as to minimize simultaneity difficulties. The lag is made considerably shorter than that on $P\dot{C}D_{L, t}$ on the assumption that product prices and consumer prices can diverge only in the short run, not in the long run.[f] Since a rise in product prices leads to increased demand for labor, which in turn tightens the labor market and adds to the upward pressure on wages and standard unit labor costs, f the sum of the

---

[d]This means that workers will be somewhat lax in seeking to shift all price increases they face as consumers back to their employers in the form of higher wages in "normal" times, but adamant about it in periods when rapid inflation is expected. Firms will also be in a weaker position to resist such worker efforts when raising prices in the latter case. On the average, workers should pass on more and absorb less of any price inflation impacts than they would in strictly "normal" times, but pass on less and absorb more than they would just in highly inflationary periods.

[e]We elected not to use the fixed weight price deflator for the private, nonfarm economy constructed by Gordon in order to facilitate comparisons among the three models we use. Our decision also has the advantage of keeping the updating of the data base and replication of our analysis by others as simple as possible. The correlation between Gordon's fixed weight price index and the implicit deflator we adopted is very close to one over our 1955:1 to 1971:2 historical period.

[f]Product prices in general and consumer prices in particular can change at different rates in the long run to the extent that relative prices shift, of course, but we abstract from these considerations here. Changes in the prices of government services are irrelevant in this regard, since they are excluded from both the product price and consumer price variables. Linking equations used later in this chapter to close the DLA model for simulation purposes show that product prices and consumer prices have indeed changed at different rates in the long run.

coefficients on the distributed lag series of product price variables is expected to be positive.

$T(E)_t$ is the one-quarter rate of change in $1/(1 - E_t)$, where E_t is the employee, or worker, tax rate defined as the proportion of personal income represented by the sum of personal tax and nontax payments plus one-half of social security contributions. In other words, $T(\dot{E})_t$ is the rate of change in the employee tax multiplier accounting for the different rates of growth that occur in the net and gross wage rates when the employee tax rate changes.[g] An increase in the tax rate workers pay reduces their net earnings for any given level of gross earnings by increasing the spread between net and gross wage rates. This results in upward pressure on wages and standard unit labor costs as the workers seek to restore the original net wage rate through gross wage increases. Accordingly, g is expected to be positive.

$T(F)_t$ is the analogue of $T(E)_t$ for employer taxes paid by firms. It is equal to the one-quarter rate of change in $1/(1 - F_t)$, where F_t is the employer, or firm, tax rate defined as the proportion of personal income represented by one-half of social security contributions. Thus, $T(F)_t$ is the rate of change in the employer tax multiplier accounting for the different rates of growth that occur in the net and gross wage rates when the employer tax rates changes. Initially an increase in the employer tax rate benefits workers, since wages are typically fixed net of employer social security contributions by wage agreements in the short run. Subsequently, however, it produces a downward pressure on the gross wage rate and standard unit labor costs as firms seek to drive unit labor costs back down to pretax change levels when wage negotiations next open. The employer tax rate variable is entered into Equation (2.1) in distributed lag form, denoted by the subscript L, to allow for this intertemporally disparate impact on gross wages. The sum of the coefficients on the distributed lag series of employer tax rate variables, h, is expected to be insignificant, reflecting the negligible combined impact of initially positive coefficients followed by negative ones.

The Price Equation

The DLA price equation is based on the hypothesis that standard unit labor costs are the main driving force behind prices. The markup of prices over unit labor costs is allowed to vary in the short run in response to changes in demand

---

[g]Letting N be the net wage, G the gross wage, and T the tax rate, $N = G(1-T)$. Thus, $G = N(1/1-T)$ and, ignoring the dynamics involved, $\%\Delta G = \%\Delta N + \%\Delta(1/1-T)$. With a fixed supply of labor, the entire burden of any tax change would be borne by labor, and the coefficient on $\%\Delta(1/1-T)$ would be zero. With a perfectly elastic supply of labor, workers would maintain their net wage by refusing to work for less, and the coefficient on $\%\Delta(1/1-T)$ would be one.

conditions and other factors, but is assumed constant in the long run owing to the constancy of labor's share of income observed in the U.S. economy. The price equation to be fitted is

$$PN\dot{F}D_t = i + j\left(\frac{\dot{W}}{Q^*}\right)_{L,t} + k\left(\frac{\dot{Q}}{Q^*}\right)_{L,t} + l\left(\frac{\dot{W}}{CMH}\right)'_t + m\left(\frac{U\dot{F}K}{UFK^*}\right)_t, \quad (2.2)$$

where the t and L subscripts and the dots above the variables have the same interpretations as in the DLA wage equation.

$PN\dot{F}D_t$, the dependent variable of Equation (2.2), is the GNP implicit price deflator for the private, nonfarm economy used to construct the labor demand price variable appearing in the wage equation. Consistent with its use in that equation, it is employed as the product prices dependent variable here. $P\dot{C}D_t$ cannot be used in this context, because it covers only a subset of the prices in the private, nonfarm economy.

$(\dot{W}/Q^*)_t$, the dependent variable of the wage equation, is included as the main explanatory variable of the wage equation, because faster standard unit labor cost growth requires more rapid price increases for profit margin maintenance. The variable appears in distributed lag form, as denoted by the L subscript, in recognition of the fact that cost increases tend to bring forth only partial price adjustments at first, owing to the "administered" pricing practices of U.S. firms, with complete adjustment coming only after a series of such delayed partial adjustments.[3] The sum of coefficients on the distributed lag series of unit labor cost variables, j, is expected to be positive and close to one, demonstrating the constant share primacy of standard labor unit costs in determining product prices in the long run. As a reflection of the same thing, the intercept term i should also be zero.

$(\dot{Q}/Q^*)_t$ is the one-quarter rate of change in the ratio of actual output per manhour to the trend value of output per manhour. Entered in distributed lag form, as denoted by the L subscript, this relative productivity variable captures the lagged effects short run fluctuations in productivity have on prices via the "administered" pricing mechanism already mentioned above. Whenever labor productivity grows more rapidly than normal, causing $(\dot{Q}/Q^*)_t$ to be positive, actual unit labor costs rise more slowly than standard unit labor costs in the short run until wage negotiations reopen, thereby at least partially and temporarily off-setting any upward pressures produced by standard unit labor costs on prices. For this reason, k, the sum of the relative productivity distributed lag coefficients is expected to be negative.

$(\dot{W}/CMH)'_t$ is equal to twenty-five percent of the four-quarter rate of change in the ratio of the fixed weight gross wage index to compensation per manhour. It is included among the explanatory variables of the price equation to take into account the many forms of compensation besides production worker wages which constitute standard unit labor costs. Following Gordon, the four-quarter version is utilized as a distributed lag proxy in order to preserve degrees of freedom when estimating the price equation.[h] However, the inverse of his original formulation is used in order to yield an expected coefficient sign for the variable consistent with the one expected for a similar variable in the imposed lag model of the following chapter. Since an increase in the ratio of wage to nonwage compensation lowers costs and eases upward pressure on prices for any given level of standard unit labor costs, l is expected to be negative.

UFK_t is the ratio of real unfilled orders to capacity in manufacturing, and UFK_t^* is the trend value of this ratio. Thus, $(U\dot{F}K/UFK^*)_t$ is the one-quarter rate of change in the detrended ratio of real unfilled orders to capacity in manufacturing. It is used as a measure of product market excess demand in the private, nonfarm economy. The detrended version is utilized to allow for exogenous long run shifts, e.g., in desired inventory and order backlog ratios. An increase in product market excess demand should lead to an increase in markups of prices over costs, as sellers raise prices and cut discounts in response to their improved market position vis-a-vis buyers, and in anticipation of higher costs as production expands with the added demand. As markups rise, the rate of price increase will accelerate. As a result, m is expected to be positive.

Empirical Estimates of the DLA Equations

Although it is desirable that simultaneous equations techniques be used in estimating the DLA model, owing to the interactions between wage Equation (2.1) and price Equation (2.2), we have relied on OLS regressions as discussed in the introductory chapter.

The Wage Equation

Our version of the wage equation for the 1955:1 to 1971:2 historical period, with t-statistics in parentheses, is

$$\left(\frac{\dot{W}}{Q^*}\right)_t = -0.0064 + 0.0129\,DU_t - 0.0029\,UD_t - 0.0559\,UH_t + 1.4410\,P\dot{C}D_{L,t}$$
$$(-2.71)\quad(1.98)\quad(-0.05)\quad(-0.88)\quad(4.49)$$

$$+\,1.1405\,(PN\dot{F}D-P\dot{C}D)_{L,t-1} + 0.0886\,T(\dot{E})_t + 1.1568\,T(\dot{F})_t' \qquad (2.3)$$
$$(3.08)(1.26)(4.90)$$

---

[h] Except for the compounding effect, one-fourth of the four-quarter rate of change in any variable is equal to the simple mean of the one-quarter rates of change in the variable for that year period.

$$\overline{R}^2 = 0.797; \quad D.W. = 2.64; \quad S.E. = 0.00189$$

where $T(\dot{F})'_t$ has replaced $T(\dot{F})_{L,t}$ to indicate that an imposed lag has been substituted for the freely estimated distributed lag specified. Individual distributed lag coefficients are reported in Table 2-1.

As the $\overline{R}^2$ shows, Equation (2.3) explains just under four-fifths of the variation corrected for degrees of freedom in the rate at which standard unit labor costs increased over the 1955:1 to 1971:2 period. Negative serial correlation of the unexplained residuals significant at the 5 percent confidence level is indicated by the Durbin-Watson statistic. Inspection of a correlation matrix for the independent variables, reproduced in Appendix C, shows that the price expectations variable is correlated with two of the labor market variables, but does not reveal any other obvious multicollinearity problems stemming from simple correlations among the explanatory variables.

All of the coefficients in Equation (2.3) display the expected signs. While the coefficient on $T(\dot{F})'_t$ is significantly positive, owing to the particular lag structure imposed, it reflects a long run net effect of the firm tax variable after four quarters of shifting incidence not significantly different from the zero total impact expected for $T(\dot{F})_{L,t}$. Nevertheless, in addition to having t-statistics biased upwards by the serial correlation of the residuals, these coefficients are disturbing in three important ways.[i]

The most crucial problem is that the sum of the distributed lag series of coefficients on the price expectations variable is 1.4410 and significantly greater than one at the 10 percent confidence level, whereas it was expected to be less than one. This raises the spectre of explosive, cumulating inflation or deflation, arising from a sequence such as the following. First, an initial change in the rate of growth in standard unit labor costs produces after a lag an approximately equal long run change in the rate of increase of product prices, since standard unit labor costs are expected to be and, as we shall see in Equation (2.5), actually are the primary, constant elasticity driving force behind prices, Next, this change in the rate of growth in product prices in turn causes an equivalent change in the rate of growth in consumer prices and price expectations after another lag, since we assume consumer prices cannot diverge from product prices in general in the long run. Finally, a second round change in the rate of growth in standard unit labor costs larger than the initial one results after yet a third lag from the effect price expectations have on standard unit labor costs. This last event starts the chain over again, and, other things equal, successive repetitions of this cycle must lead to ever increasing rates of inflation or deflation.

---

[i]Inasmuch as the residuals of Equation (2.4) are negatively autocorrelated, the upwards bias of the coefficient t-statistics is probably not too severe. See [21, pp. 246-249].

We are unable to account for the discrepancy between our explosive results and Gordon's stable ones with respect to the impact of price expectations. Although we have modified the DLA wage equation by including the price expectations lag in it directly and estimating it with one-quarter length observations, neither of these changes can explain our destabilizing price expectations impact. Slight differences in time spans covered and between the data bases used offer other possible, but implausible resolutions of the issue. In our view the most likely explanation rests with the specification of an unusually long six-year distributed lag pattern which results in unstable coefficient estimates.[j]

The second problem concerns DU_t, UD_t, and UH_t, which are used to show how labor market tightness affects the rate at which standard unit labor costs rise. These three variables are meant to capture changes in the labor force which, because they are more complex than fluctuations in the level of unemployment, cannot be caught simply by using a variable on the official unemployment rate. Unfortunately, of the three variables only DU_t has an impact in Equation (2.3) significantly different from zero in a two-tailed test even at the 10 percent confidence level. This suggests that the labor market variables may not be optimally formulated in the DLA wage equation.

Replacing these three variables with $(1/U)_t$, where U_t is the official unemployment rate for the civilian labor force expressed as a decimal, yields a modified DLA wage equation which can be compared to Equation (2.3). The inverse of the unemployment rate is utilized to approximate the convex impact a number of previous Phillips curve studies have found unemployment to have on the rate of increase in wages.[4] The coefficient on this unemployment inverse is expected to be positive, since a decrease in the unemployment rate and an increase in its reciprocal tightens the labor market and puts upwards pressure on wages and standard unit labor costs.

The modified DLA wage equation, with t-statistics in parentheses, is

$$\left(\frac{\dot{W}}{Q^*}\right)_t = -0.0091 + 0.0003 \left(\frac{1}{U}\right)_t + 1.6406 \, \dot{PCD}_{L,t} + 0.4355 \, (P\dot{NFD} - \dot{PCD})_{L,t-1}$$
$$ (-4.61) \quad (3.28) (8.95) (1.38)$$

$$+ 0.0718 \, T(\dot{E})_t + 1.1496 \, T(\dot{F})_t' \tag{2.4}$$
$$ (0.97) (4.81)$$

$$\bar{R}^2 = 0.787; \quad \text{D.W.} = 2.42; \quad \text{S.E.} = 0.00194$$

Individual lag coefficients are reported in Table 2-1.

---

[j]Gordon also estimated the price expectations lag directly in the wage equation using one-quarter length observations, but did not find a destabilizing price expectations effect. See [19, pp. 396-397]. Our historical period begins four quarters later and ends two quarters later than Gordon's sample period. Regressions run over subsets of the 1955:1 to

Table 2-1
Individual Distributed Lag Coefficients for Equations (2.3), (2.4), and (2.5)
(with t-statistics in parentheses)

Period	Equation (2.3)		Equation (2.4)		Equation (2.5)	
	$\dot{PCD}_{L,t}$	$(P\dot{NFD}-\dot{PCD})_{L,t-1}$	$\dot{PCD}_{L,t}$	$(P\dot{NFD}-\dot{PCD})_{L,t-1}$	$\left(\dfrac{\dot{w}}{Q^*}\right)_{L,t}$	$\left(\dfrac{\dot{Q}}{Q^*}\right)_{L,t}$
t	0.0586 (0.64)		0.0670 (0.79)	0.1029 (1.03)	0.2718 (2.81)	−0.1341 (−4.02)
$t-1$	0.0917 (1.54)	0.1553 (1.63)	0.1078 (2.31)	0.1264 (1.85)	0.2131 (3.63)	−0.0436 (−1.64)
$t-2$	0.1116 (2.75)	0.2030 (2.94)	0.1312 (5.52)	0.0833 (1.32)	0.1608 (2.60)	−0.0253 (−1.01)
$t-3$	0.1207 (3.74)	0.1650 (2.51)	0.1409 (7.24)	0.0302 (0.53)	0.1161 (2.24)	−0.0339 (−1.48)
$t-4$	0.1216 (4.06)	0.1156 (1.91)	0.1398 (5.74)	0.0007 (0.01)	0.0797 (1.33)	−0.0397 (−1.65)
$t-5$	0.1162 (4.02)	0.0962 (1.46)	0.1311 (4.72)	0.0060 (0.10)	0.0518 (0.77)	−0.0291 (−1.24)
$t-6$	0.1065 (3.92)	0.1155 (1.72)	0.1171 (4.16)	0.0344 (0.53)	0.0317 (0.58)	−0.0043 (−0.16)
$t-7$	0.0941 (3.83)	0.1493 (1.99)	0.1003 (3.82)	0.0515 (0.74)	0.0186 (0.44)	0.0168 (0.63)
$t-8$	0.0805 (3.72)	0.1407 (1.87)	0.0825 (3.54)		0.0105 ( )	
$t-9$	0.0669 (3.47)		0.0653 (3.20)		0.00	
$t-10$	0.0543 (3.02)		0.0500 (2.71)			
$t-11$	0.0434 (2.46)		0.0377 (2.13)			

$t-12$	0.0349 (1.96)			0.0288 (1.63)		
$t-13$	0.0290 (1.63)			0.0239 (1.36)		
$t-14$	0.0258 (1.49)			0.0229 (1.35)		
$t-15$	0.0251 (1.53)			0.0254 (1.61)		
$t-16$	0.0266 (1.70)			0.0309 (2.14)		
$t-17$	0.0298 (1.88)			0.0384 (2.75)		
$t-18$	0.0337 (1.95)			0.0466 (3.09)		
$t-19$	0.0374 (1.91)			0.0540 (3.08)		
$t-20$	0.0396 (1.84)			0.0586 (2.93)		
$t-21$	0.0388 (1.77)			0.0582 (2.78)		
$t-22$	0.0333 (1.71)			0.0529 (2.65)		
$t-23$	0.0210 (1.66)			0.0320 (2.55)		
Mean Lag	8.2678	3.2627		8.6434	2.2590	1.9938	1.3936
Sum of Coefficients	1.4410 (4.49)	1.1405 (3.08)		1.6406 (8.95)	0.4355 (1.38)	0.9595 (6.54)	−0.2933 (−2.06)

Source: Authors' estimates.

Note: All lags are fourth-degree polynomial Almon lags with the lag coefficient constrained to zero in the period immediately preceding in time the far period in the lag. The lagged coefficients of 1.0, −0.50, −0.33, −0.17 on $\dot{T}(F)_t'$ are not listed, because they are imposed rather than estimated.

Equation (2.4) differs noticeably from Equation (2.3) in two ways: price expectations have a larger, more significant impact, while the difference between product prices in general and consumer prices in particular has a smaller, now insignificant one in the new, modified equation. The Durbin-Watson test for autocorrelation is now inconclusive.

It has been argued that much of the inflation which occurred during our 1955:1 to 1971:2 historical period can be explained either on the basis of inflationary expectations or on that of shifts in the composition of the labor force, owing to the lack of sufficient evidence to distinguish between these separate hypotheses. Such an argument implies that the optimum formulation of labor market variables in a wage equation is likely to depend greatly on which of these two approaches is taken, how the equation is specified, and what other variables are included.[5] Given the nearly identical explanatory power revealed by their summary statistics, Equations (2.3) and (2.4) on the surface appear to confirm this view. Yet, as we shall see in the next section, simulation of the DLA model with each of these two equations leads to quite different results, when considering the overall inflation process as opposed to the behavior of standard unit labor costs alone.

The third major coefficient problem with Equation (2.3) rests with the distributed lag coefficients of the firm tax variable. Although we were able to obtain sensible results using a distributed lag on the rate of change in the firm tax rate itself, none of a variety of lag structures—including no lag and a single-period lag—made sense when we used the multiplier form of the firm tax variable specified a priori. Lags freely estimated with this multiplier formulation invariably implied more than 100 percent shifting of the tax incidence, and in two directions more often than not. Consequently, we have constrained the lag coefficients to 1.0, −0.5, −0.33, and −0.17 in the four periods t through $t-3$, respectively, as Gordon was forced to do in his original application of the model. Based on the need to make this restriction, we question whether the tax variables as currently defined serve as independent variables in themselves or as proxies for some other unrecognized influence.[6]

The Price Equation

Our estimate of the DLA price equation for the historical period 1955:1 to 1971:2, with t-statistics in parentheses, is

1971:2 period, for tests on the structural stability of the wage equation described later in this chapter, yielded sums of the distributed lag price expectations coefficients which varied widely between 2.4007 and 6.4477. Some were statistically significant; others were insignificant. Test regressions run for the entire 1955:1 to 1971:2 period with alternative length lags on price expectations exhibited total price expectations impacts which declined as the lag was shortened; the sum of the lag coefficients was 0.7438 using a lag of eight quarters, for instance, lowering the $\bar{R}^2$ by 0.042 to 0.755. For other comments on Gordon's use of such an unusually long price expectations lag, see [18, pp. 159-164].

$$PN\dot{F}D_t = 0.0009 + 0.9595\left(\frac{\dot{W}}{Q^*}\right)_{L,t} - 0.2933\left(\frac{\dot{Q}}{Q^*}\right)_{L,t} - 0.4246\left(\frac{\dot{W}}{CMH}\right)_t'$$
$$\phantom{PN\dot{F}D_t =} (1.23) \quad (6.54) \phantom{\left(\frac{\dot{W}}{Q^*}\right)_{L,t}} (-2.06) \phantom{\left(\frac{\dot{Q}}{Q^*}\right)} (-2.26)$$

$$+ 0.0249\ \frac{U\dot{F}K}{UFK^*}_t \qquad\qquad (2.5)$$
$$ (2.52)$$

$$\overline{R}^2 = 0.733; \quad D.W. = 2.40; \quad S.E. = 0.00208$$

Individual distributed lag coefficients for the equation are reported in Table 2-1.

Equation (2.5) requires very little comment. It explains 73 percent of the variation corrected for degrees of freedom in the rate at which product prices increased over the historical period. There is no serial correlation of the residuals according to the Durbin-Watson statistic. Inspection of a correlation matrix of the independent variables, reproduced in Appendix C, reveals no multicollinearity problems.

All coefficients have the expected sign and are significant in two-tailed tests at the 5 percent confidence level, except the constant term which is insignificant as expected. Standard unit labor costs have the unit elasticity long run impacts expected: the 0.9595 sum of the series of lag coefficients is significantly positive and not significantly different from one. The variable $(\dot{W}/CMH)_t'$ appears to work marginally better than did the original, reciprocal version in preliminary analyses, but this may simply reflect data revisions.[7]

Stability Tests

We have evaluated the structural stability of Equations (2.3) through (2.5) over the period 1955:1 to 1971:2 by dividing that time span into three subperiods, estimating the equations for each of the subperiods, and then computing tests of equality on the subperiod regressions. Both of the wage equations are unstable for the 1955:1–1965:1 and 1966:1–1971:2 subperiod comparisons, but stable otherwise. The price equation is stable for all subperiods tested. Table 2-2 summarizes the results of these stability tests, which are considered in greater detail in Chapter 5.

Simulation and Mathematical Solution of the DLA Model

Owing to the interactions that occur between wages and prices, how well the DLA model protrays the dynamics of the inflation process can only be judged by considering the DLA wage and price equations jointly. We have simulated the DLA model for the 1955:1 to 1971:2 period using both Equations (2.3) and

Table 2-2
F-Statistics from Tests of Equality on the DLA Wage and Price Equations across Subsets of the 1955:1 to 1971:2 Period
(with degrees of freedom in parentheses)

	Subperiods Tested		
	1955:1 to 1960:4 and 1961:1 to 1965:4	1955:1 to 1965:4 and 1966:1 to 1971:2	1955:1 to 1960:4, 1961:1 to 1965:4, and 1966:1 to 1971:2
Wage Equation (2.3)	0.79 (14,16)	1.99 (14,38)*	1.09 (28,24)
Modified Wage Equation (2.4)	1.36 (12,20)	2.24 (12,42)*	1.53 (24,30)
Price Equation (2.5)	0.98 (11,22)	1.19 (11,44)	1.04 (22,33)

Source: Authors' estimates.

Note: For a discussion of the procedures used to compute these F-statistics, see [8], [19], and [21, pp. 192-208].

*F-statistic significant at the 5 percent confidence level, but not at the 1 percent confidence level.

(2.4) as the wage equation, and solved for the long run Phillips curve tradeoff implied by the model under equilibrium assumptions employing Equation (2.4) as the wage equation. The degree to which the simulations capture the actual behavior of wages and prices, provides an indirect measure of how serious are the bias problems introduced by our use of OLS regressions in estimating the DLA equations, in spite of the wage and price simultaneity involved.

Simulation Results

For simulations of the DLA model to completely capture the effects fed back by wages and prices onto each other, all wage and price variables must be endogenously determined within the model. For both the standard unit labor cost and product price variables, the main wage variable and one of two main price variables, respectively, this is the case. However, for $(\dot{W}/CMH)'_t$ and the price expectations variable using the rate of change in the consumption expenditures deflator this is not the case.

We believe a strong argument can be made for treating $(\dot{W}/CMH)'_t$ as an endogenous variable, since it contains the fixed weight gross wage index and compensation per manhour, both of which are closely related to the endogenous standard unit labor costs variable. However, the simulation results described here are based on the assumption that $(\dot{W}/CMH)'_t$ is exogenous. We have made this assumption to maintain consistency with Gordon's analysis and to simplify comparisons with results presented for our other models in the next two chapters.[k]

Making a similar assumption about the price expectations variable being exogenous would be inappropriate, for it is much more central to the analysis, particularly given the destabilizing role it plays in the wage equation. We have closed the model with respect to price expectations by introducing into the simulations another separate equation linking the rate of change in the consumption expenditures deflator to an eight-quarter distributed lag on past rates of change in the private, nonfarm economy deflator. This linking equation, based on the same fourth degree polynomial lag used in the wage and price equations, was estimated for the peak-to-peak period 1949:1 to 1969:1 in order to avoid business cycle influences and take into account the pre-1955 importance of consumer prices stemming from the six year lag on price expectations. The equation is

$$\dot{PCD}_t = 0.0008 + 0.8647\,P\dot{N}FD_t + 0.1122\,P\dot{N}FD_{t-1} - 0.0880\,P\dot{N}FD_{t-2}$$
$$(1.08)(12.67)(2.46)(-2.26)$$

$$- 0.0430\,P\dot{N}FD_{t-3} + 0.0384\,P\dot{N}FD_{t-4} + 0.0459\,P\dot{N}FD_{t-5}$$
$$(-1.67)(1.10)(1.58)$$

$$- 0.0322\,P\dot{N}FD_{t-6} - 0.1092\,P\dot{N}FD_{t-7}\,. (2.6)$$
$$(-1.17)(-2.62)$$

$$\overline{R}^2 = 0.738;\ \ D.W. = 1.76;\ \ S.E. = 0.00297$$

The sum of the lag coefficients is 0.7888, with a standard error of 0.1198. This sum is just barely significantly less than one in a one-tailed test at the 5 percent confidence level, demonstrating that product prices in general and consumer prices in particular can diverge to a modest degree in the long run.[l]

In simulating the DLA model we have found the rate of change in the fixed

---

[k]Treating $(\dot{W}/CMH)_t$ as endogenous raises the problem of explaining CMH_t. In preliminary simulations of the DLA model we found it extremely difficult to explain CMH_t satisfactorily without using a full-blown wage equation or simply linking it back to $\dot{W}_t$, much as we do in solving for the long run Phillips curve later in this chapter. Our preliminary simulations with $(\dot{W}/CMH)_t'$ handled endogenously did not appear to work any better than those with it handled exogenously.

[l]In actually performing the simulations $\dot{PCD}_t$, and all other variables, are treated as exogenous for periods prior to 1955. Reestimating Equation (2.6) for the period 1949:1 to 1971:2 had a minor impact on it and left the sum of the lagged coefficients significantly less than one at the 5 percent confidence level. Reestimating a similar equation for the 1955:1 to 1971:2 period raised the sum of the coefficients, leaving it less than one by an insignificant amount. For other evidence on the relationship between the rates of change in product prices in general and consumer prices in particular, see [12, p. 28], [18, p. 121], and our discussion of the ILA model simulation, particularly footnote h, in Chapter 3.

weight gross wage index, $\dot{W}_t$, rather than in standard unit labor costs. Inasmuch as Q_t^* grows at a constant rate owing to the way it is defined, this transformation requires merely that a constant be subtracted from the simulated value of $(\dot{W}/Q^*)_t$ and introduces no distortion other than a rounding error. Making the transformation facilitates comparisons and our analysis for two reasons: $\dot{W}_t$ is the dependent variable of the wage equation in the other models we use; Phase II regulations placed a ceiling on wages, not on standard unit labor costs.[8]

Figure 2-1 traces out the one-quarter rates of change in gross wages and product prices on a quarterly basis as they actually occurred during the 1955:1 to 1971:2 period and as simulated by the DLA model with each of the two alternative DLA wage equations. Table 2-3 reports a number of error measures for the simulations. The light lines in Figure 2-2 relate the changes in product prices to the unemployment rate on an annual basis for actual movements and the modified wage equation simulation.

Although the wage equation containing DU_t, UD_t, and UH_t explains slightly more of the variation in the rate at which standard unit labor costs rose during the 1955:1 to 1971:2 period than does the modified one containing $(1/U)_t$ when the wage equations are examined in isolation, it does not perform as well in simulating the overall wage-price behavior of the economy. For, Figure 2-1 and Table 2-3 plainly show that the DLA model simulation using Equation (2.4) works markedly better than the one using Equation (2.3). At least within the DLA model, price expectations offer a superior explanation for recent inflation compared with shifts in the composition of the labor market when wage and price feedback dynamics are considered, even though the two hypotheses work about equally well when wages are considered by themselves.

Both simulations overpredict the rates of change in wages and prices on the average, as the negative mean errors in Table 2-3 attest. However, the wage Equation (2.3) simulation overprediction is consistent and cumulates over time, while this is not the case with the smaller overprediction of the modified wage Equation (2.4) simulation. The difference can be seen directly in Figure 2-1 and indirectly from the larger absolute magnitude of every wage Equation (2.3) simulation error measure relative to its modified wage Equation (2.4) simulation counterpart in Table 2-3. It is also reflected in the Table 2-3 regressions of the actual rates of change in wages and prices on the simulated rates of change in them. Ideally, such regressions should have intercepts equal to zero and coefficients on the independent variable equal to one for deterministic simulations such as ours.[9] The hypothesis that the regressions based on the modified wage Equation (2.4) simulation have these properties cannot be rejected; the hypothesis that the regressions based on the Equation (2.3) simulation have them cannot be sustained.

The modified wage equation simulation correctly identifies most major turning points in the movements of wages and prices despite overpredicting on

25

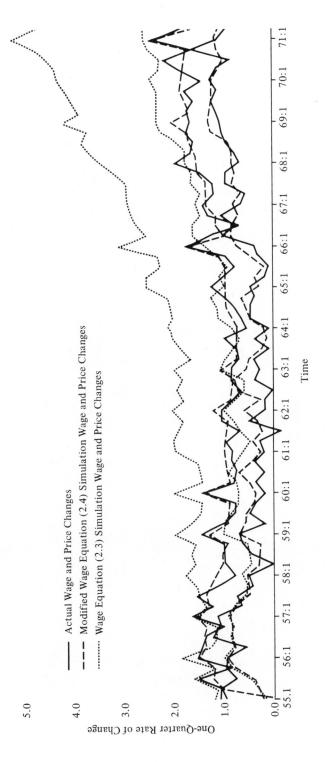

One-Quarter Rate of Change

5.0
4.0
3.0
2.0
1.0
0.0

55:1 56:1 57:1 58:1 59:1 60:1 61:1 62:1 63:1 64:1 65:1 66:1 67:1 68:1 69:1 70:1 71:1

Time

——— Actual Wage and Price Changes
– – – Modified Wage Equation (2.4) Simulation Wage and Price Changes
········· Wage Equation (2.3) Simulation Wage and Price Changes

Figure 2-1. 1955:1 to 1971:2 Wage and Price Changes as They Actually Occurred and as Simulated with the DLA Model.

Table 2-3
Error Measures for the 1955:1 to 1971:2 DLA Model Simulations

	Simulation using wage Equation (2.3)	Simulation using wage Equation (2.4)
$\dot{w}_t$		
Mean Error	−0.0123581	−0.000416666
Root Mean Square Error	0.0148448	0.00195670
Mean Absolute Error	0.0125076	0.00152937
Theil U Statistic	0.378992	0.076829
Regression of actual on simulated values	$\dot{w}_t = 0.0051 + 0.2814\ \hat{\dot{w}}_t$ $(5.62) \quad (8.24)$ $\overline{R}^2 = 0.507$	$\dot{w}_t = -0.0012 + 1.0621\ \hat{\dot{w}}_t$ $(-1.37) \quad (15.76)$ $\overline{R}^2 = 0.792$
$P\dot{N}FD_t$		
Mean Error	−0.00592877	−0.000232183
Root Mean Square Error	0.00750554	0.00211660
Mean Absolute Error	0.00640130	0.00169993
Theil U Statistic	0.360682	0.148025
Regression of actual on simulated values	$P\dot{N}FD_t = 0.0008 + 0.4397\ P\hat{\dot{N}}FD_t$ $(1.04) \quad (8.25)$ $\overline{R}^2 = 0.508$	$P\dot{N}FD_t = -0.0003 + 1.0061\ P\hat{\dot{N}}FD_t$ $(-0.49) \quad (12.95)$ $\overline{R}^2 = 0.720$

Source: Authors' estimates.

Note: The mean of $\dot{W}_t$ is 0.0119209; the mean of $P\dot{N}FD_t$ is 0.0059960. The error measures are calculated according to the following formulae, where A_t denotes the actual value, P_t the value predicted by the simulation, and T the number of observations contained in the simulation interval:

$$\text{mean error} = \frac{1}{T} \sum_{t=1}^{T} (A_t - P_t); \quad \text{root mean square error} = \sqrt{\frac{1}{T} \sum_{t=1}^{T} (A_t - P_t)^2};$$

$$\text{mean absolute error} = \frac{1}{T} \sum_{t=1}^{T} |A_t - P_t|;$$

$$\text{Theil U statistic} = \frac{\sqrt{\frac{1}{T} \sum_{t=1}^{T} (A_t - P_t)^2}}{\sqrt{\frac{1}{T} \sum_{t=1}^{T} A_t^2} + \sqrt{\frac{1}{T} \sum_{t=1}^{T} P_t^2}}.$$

The Theil U statistic is bounded by zero and one, taking on the value zero in the case of a perfect forecast. Its properties are described in [46, pp. 31-34]. For a description of the properties which a regression of dependent variable actual on simulated values has for deterministic simulations such as ours, see [1] and [9].

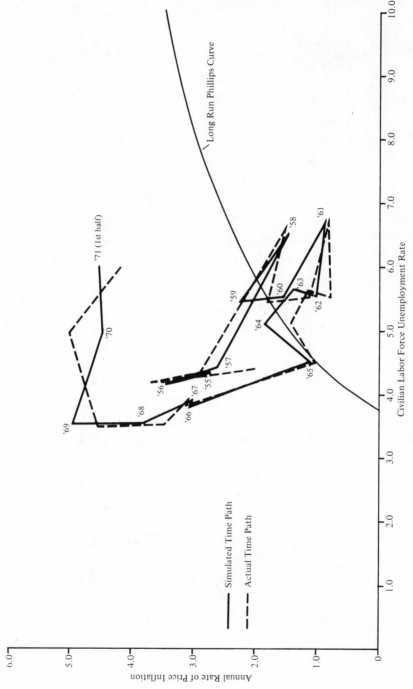

Figure 2-2. Long Run Phillips Curve and Simulated Time Path of the Economy for the DLA Model Using Wage Equation (2.4).

the average. This can perhaps best be seen by comparing in Figure 2-2 the actual path of unemployment-inflation experiences traced out by the economy with the wage Equation (2.4) simulation path. The ability of the modified DLA model simulation to track turning points so well, despite the potential for explosive inflation noted earlier in connection with the wage equation price expectations impact, can be attributed to two things. First, movements in product prices are not completely transmitted to consumer prices as hypothesized, since the sum of the lag coefficients linking PCD_t to $PNFD_t$ in Equation (2.6) is less than one. Second, changes occurred in various exogenous variables during the 1955:1 to 1972:2 period which drove standard unit labor costs and prices down enough to offset the explosive impacts price expectations had. That the original wage equation simulation has a cumulating error and does not do nearly as well in pinpointing turning points can only be attributed to the substitution of supplementary measures of labor market tightness for the unemployment rate inverse in the wage equation.

Long Run Phillips Curve

The long run tradeoff between unemployment and inflation implied by the DLA model can be determined by simultaneously solving the wage and price equations after making appropriate steady state assumptions. Using Equations (2.4) and (2.5), we have found this tradeoff assuming:

1. all prices change in the same proportion;

2. tax rates are constant;

3. product market excess demand conditions are constant;

4. the ratio of the fixed weight gross wage index to compensation per manhour declines at the rate of 0.2 percent a year; and

5. wages, prices, and productivity have been growing at their constant, steady state rates long enough for initial conditions and lag structures to have no impacts.[m]

We have chosen to derive the Phillips curve for wage Equation (2.4) rather than for Equation (2.3), although the latter was originally specified as the wage equation, because the former worked better in the simulations. Moreover, use of the latter equation would require complex transformations based on what we consider untenable assumptions to explain DU_t, UD_t, and UH_t as functions of the official unemployment rate.[10]

---

[m]The fourth assumption regarding the rate of change in the ratio of the fixed weight gross wage index to compensation per manhour is taken directly from Gordon's original analysis of the DLA model. See [18, p. 136]. Taking account of the fact that Gordon used $(C\dot{M}H/W)'_t$ while we use $(\dot{W}/CMH)'_t$, leads to a small rounding error we have ignored and the sign reversal we have made.

The heavy line in Figure 2-2 represents the long run Phillips curve implied by the DLA model under the assumptions listed above. Its positive slope, clearly anomalous in the context of Phillips curve tradeoffs identified by other studies, stems from the greater than unitary long run impact which price expectations have in the wage equation and reflects the potential for explosive, cumulating inflation described earlier. Replacing wage Equation (2.4) with wage Equation (2.3) when solving for the Phillips curve would not eliminate the anomaly, since price expectations have a destabilizing impact in that equation too.

The steady state tradeoffs between unemployment and inflation implied by the DLA model are unstable. Were the economy perturbed while in one of these steady states, it would not return to either the same or another steady state position according to the DLA model. Rather, inflation would either accelerate or decelerate indefinitely, depending on whether the initial impact on prices was positive or negative.

Each annual unemployment-inflation experience depicted by the light lines time path in Figure 2-2 can be thought of as a point on a particular short run Phillips curve, flatter than the long run curve, that shifts about the long run curve from one year to the next.

3 An Imposed Lag Adjustment Model

The imposed lag adjustment (ILA) model described in this chapter was set forth by Otto Eckstein and Roger Brinner in a study prepared for the Joint Economic Committee of Congress.[1] Inasmuch as Eckstein and Brinner drew heavily on the earlier work of Gordon used as the basis for our DLA model, it closely resembles the DLA model discussed in the preceding chapter. The key changes Eckstein and Brinner incorporated in the ILA model were the imposition of a fixed lag structure, the introduction of a nonlinear price expectations effect, and the measurement of labor market conditions with the official unemployment rate inverse as opposed to a more complex set of variables. In addition, they altered the specifications of several other variables. Most of the data transformations introduced by Gordon were maintained.

We have made only one modification in applying the ILA model. Whereas Eckstein and Brinner estimated the wage equation with overlapping four-quarter rate of change observations, we have used one-quarter rate of change observations to facilitate comparisons among the three models we estimate.

Specification of the ILA Model

The imposed lag adjustment model consists of a wage equation and a price equation, which model the inflation process in an explicitly simultaneous manner by recognizing the interactions wages and prices have on one another. Complete definitions of all variables and descriptions of all data sources used in the model are contained in Appendixes A and B, respectively.

The Wage Equation

The ILA wage equation is eclectic as is the DLA wage equation in that it includes a variety of variables other studies have found to affect wages, rather than including only certain variables intended to test a particular theory of wage determination. The wage equation to be fitted is

$$\dot{W}_t = a + b\left(\frac{1}{U}\right)_t + c\,\dot{PCD}_t + d\,\dot{JP}_t + e\,T(\dot{E})_t' + f\,GP_t. \tag{3.1}$$

31

The t subscripts refer to quarter-year time periods. A bar appears over a variable to denote its utilization in an imposed lag form; unless explicitly stated to the contrary, the imposed lag has the standard weights 0.4, 0.3, 0.2, 0.1 for the time periods t through t-3, implying a complete long run adjustment summing to one within one year.

$\dot{W}_t$, the dependent variable of Equation (3.1), is the one-quarter rate of change in the fixed weight gross wage index, including fringe benefits and adjusted for interindustry employment shifts and manufacturing overtime, paid to production workers in the private, nonfarm economy. This is the same wage index used in the DLA model as the numerator of standard unit labor costs.

$(1/U)_t$ is the reciprocal of the civilian labor force unemployment rate, where that rate is expressed in decimal form. It was chosen by Eckstein and Brinner as the measure of labor market tightness, after they concluded from tests that more complicated measures of labor market tightness failed to explain wages any better.[2] The inverse of the unemployment rate is used, instead of the unemployment rate itself, to approximate the convex relationship between the latter variable and the rate of change in wages remarked upon in conjunction with the alternate DLA wage equation of the preceding chapter.[3] Since a fall in the unemployment rate and a rise in its inverse tightens the labor market, thereby putting additional upward pressure on wages, the rate of change in wages should rise when $(1/U)_t$ rises. Accordingly, b is expected to be positive.

Two variables in Equation (3.1) measure price expectations based on the hypothesis that workers form price expectations about future inflation by extrapolating past inflation experience with respect to the prices they pay as consumers. $\dot{PCD}_t$ is the one-quarter rate of change in the GNP implicit price deflator for personal consumption expenditures. It is used in a standard imposed lag, denoted by the bar over it, to capture the "normal" impact price expectations have on wages. JP_t is an inflation severity variable, zero in "normal" times when consumer prices have risen 5 percent or less over the preceding two years and equal to $(\dot{PCD}_t + \ldots + \dot{PCD}_{t-7}) - 0.05$ in inflationary times when consumer prices have risen more than 5 percent over the preceding two years.[a] It is used to capture the extra impact price expectations have on wages in addition to their "normal" impact during periods of rapid inflation.

In "normal" times, defined here as any period when consumer prices have risen on average no more than 2.5 percent per annum over the last two years, workers perceive and experience relatively little real wage reduction as inflation

---

[a]Using $(\dot{PCD} + \ldots + \dot{PCD}_{t-7}) - 0.05$ greater than zero as the inflation severity cutoff criterion is not exactly the same as using the criterion that consumer prices be 5 percent or more higher than two years ago owing to the different frequency of compounding, but this difference and the rounding error associated with it are minor for so short a period.

eats into their money wages. Consequently, they have small incentive when bargaining with employers to insist on obtaining money wage supplements proportionate to the future rate of inflation expected as a means of maintaining their real wages. Rather, they settle for a less than proportionate increase in their money wages, perhaps passing on part of their purchasing power loss to their employers, but absorbing most themselves. Since $\overline{P\dot{C}D}_t$ reflects this "normal," inelastic labor supply adjustment process, its coefficient c is expected to be positive but less than one. Implicit in its use is the notion that "normal" price expectations adapt to actual experience within one year, a far cry from the six years needed in the DLA model.

When inflation occurs more rapidly than "normal," the diminution of workers' purchasing power mounts correspondingly and is more readily perceived by workers. As a consequence, workers form more inflationary price expectations and become more adamant about maintaining their real wages through higher money wages, for more is at stake. Since $J\dot{P}_t$ reflects the increment of price expectations above "normal" levels leading to this tougher bargaining stance on the part of workers, d is expected to be positive. It is expected to be less than one, however, because the maintenance of workers' real wages requires increases in their money wages proportionate to the rate of inflation and their "normal" efforts towards this end are already captured by $P\dot{C}D_t$ and its positive coefficient. Implicit in the use of $J\dot{P}_t$ is the notion that workers' price expectations take two years, or twice as long as "normal," to adapt completely to unusually rapid inflation.

As in the DLA model, $T(E)_t$ is the one-quarter rate of change in $1/(1 - E_t)$, where E_t is the employee tax rate defined as the proportion of personal income represented by the sum of personal tax and nontax payments plus one-half of social security contributions. However, here it is used as $\overline{T(E)}_t'$ with an imposed lag of standard length but nonstandard weights 10.0, −4.5, −3.0, −1.5, as the bar over it and the prime after it denote, to capture the offsetting effects that an employee tax rate change has on gross wages as time elapses.[b] An increase in the employee tax rate initially places upward pressure on the gross wage rate by driving a wedge between net and gross wages and raising the gross wage needed to maintain a given net wage. Whatever gross wage rate increase workers are initially able to bargain for in attempting to maintain their net wage, must subsequently put downward pressure on the gross wage rate as firms seek to

---

[b]While the intent is different, in practice $\overline{T(E)}_t'$ is likely to catch basically the same effects that $T(\dot{E})_t$ and $T(\dot{F})_{L,t}$ were designed to capture in combination in the DLA model. According to Eckstein and Brinner, they excluded some form of variable analogous to $T(\dot{F})_t$ from the ILA wage equation only after finding it insignificant. See [12, p. 17] and our discussion in the previous chapter of the problems encountered in obtaining empirical estimates of the impact of $\overline{T(F)}_{L,t}$ in the DLA wage equation.

eliminate the increase in their unit labor costs produced by the higher wage rate. The specification of the imposed lag coefficients implies that firms are able to shift back to workers within three quarters of a year 90 percent of the gross wage rate increase that workers initially obtain following an increase in the employee tax rate. A value for e in excess of 0.1 would imply more than 100 percent initial backward shifting of employee tax rate changes onto employers, given the imposed lag coefficient chosen for the current quarter. Inasmuch as workers are probably able to temporarily shift some, but not all of an employee tax rate increase on to their employers by reducing the amount of the supply, e is expected to be positive but quite small.

GP_t is a dummy variable designed to measure the degree to which the wage-price guideposts held down wages during the mid-1960s. GP_t rises linearly from 0.25 in 1962:1 to 1.0 in 1962:4, stays at that level until 1966:4 and then falls linearly back to zero in 1967:4, as a characterization of the hypothesized wage-price guideline impact pattern. Figure 3-1 pictures this time path of values. The coefficient f is expected to be negative, reflecting a guidelines impact which slowed the rate of wage inflation.[c]

The Price Equation

The ILA price equation is very similar to the DLA price equation. It too is based on the hypothesis that labor costs are the main driving force behind prices, with labor's share of income remaining constant in the long run as changes in unit labor costs are passed on in the form of equiproportionate price changes. It recognizes the same major influences as determinants of the rate of change in prices. Only the precise specification of the particular variables representing these influences is changed.

The ILA price equation to be fitted is

$$PN\dot{F}D_t = g + h\,(\bar{\dot{W}}_{t-1} - 0.0065) + i\,(\dot{W}_t - \bar{\dot{W}}_{t-1}) + j\,(\bar{\dot{Q}}_{t-1} - 0.0065)$$
$$+ k\,(\dot{Q}_t - \bar{\dot{Q}}_{t-1}) + l\,(\bar{\dot{W}}_t - \overline{CMH}_t) + m\,(UFK_t - UFK_{t-1})' \quad (3.2)$$

where the t subscripts and the bars and dots above variables have the same meanings as in the ILA wage equation.

The dependent variable of price Equation (3.2), $PN\dot{F}D_t$, is the one-quarter

---

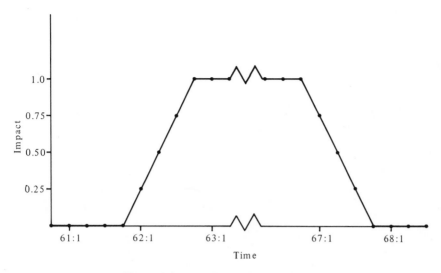

Figure 3-1. Time Path of GP_t Values.

rate of change in the GNP implicit price deflator for the private, nonfarm economy. It does not appear in the ILA wage equation, since no product price variable is used there.

The number 0.0065 represents the trend value of the one-quarter rate of growth in output per manhour, or productivity, as originally estimated by Eckstein and Brinner for the private, nonfarm economy.[4] It corresponds to Q_t^* in the DLA model. Our own estimates of this magnitude ranged between 0.0063 and 0.0067 for a variety of postwar periods, including our 1955:1 to 1971:2 estimation period, so we have retained the original value 0.0065. ($\dot{\bar{W}}_{t-1}$ − 0.0065) represents the long run one-quarter rate or change in standard unit labor costs, defined as the difference between the long run rate of change in wages and the long run rate of change in labor productivity. It is the main factor determining the rate of change in prices. $\dot{W}_t$, the one-quarter rate of change in the fixed weight gross wage index, is taken from the ILA wage equation and used in a standard imposed lag, denoted by the bar over it, beginning in the previous quarter as the long run weighted average rate of change in wages. The long run rate of change in labor productivity, 0.0065, is then subtracted to yield the long run rate of change in standard unit labor costs. For labor's share of income to remain constant in the long run, unit labor cost changes must be passed on in the form of equiproportionate price changes. Consequently, h is expected to take on a positive value approximately equal to one and the constant term g is expected to be zero.

($\dot{W}_t - \dot{\bar{W}}_{t-1}$) measures the difference between the current one-quarter rate of change in the fixed weight gross wage index and the weighted average, long run rate of change in it. $(\dot{W}_t - \overline{\dot{W}}_{t-1})$ is positive when the current rate of wage growth temporarily exceeds the long run rate in the short run and negative in the opposite case. It is included as an explanatory variable to capture the extra upward pressure not captured in standard unit labor costs that operates on actual unit labor costs and prices whenever wages rise faster than usual in the short run. The coefficient i is expected to be positive as a relection of this pressure, but less than one owing to the partial adjustment lag of price to costs involved in the previously discussed "administered" pricing process.[5]

$\dot{Q}_t$ is the current one-quarter rate of change in output per manhour in the private, nonfarm economy. Since 0.0065 represents its long run trend value, $(\overline{\dot{Q}}_{t-1} - 0.0065)$ and $(\dot{Q}_t - \overline{\dot{Q}}_{t-1})$ must be interpreted not only in relation to each other, but also in relation to 0.0065. $(\overline{\dot{Q}}_{t-1} - 0.0065)$, the difference between the standard lag form of the productivity rate of change variable and its long run value in the previous period, can be viewed as the deviation between the rates of productivity growth in the intermediate and long runs. By analogy $(\dot{Q}_t - \overline{\dot{Q}}_{t-1})$ then becomes the deviation between the rates of productivity growth in the short and intermediate runs. When productivity rises faster than usual in either the intermediate or short run, upward pressures on prices are temporarily alleviated to the extent that increases in other elements of unit costs are offset. Both j and k are expected to be negative as a reflection of this impact. Owing to the lags involved in the "administered" pricing practices of U.S. firms and the inclusion of long run productivity changes in Equation (3.2) via the standard unit labor cost variable, the absolute values of these two coefficients should sum to less than one, with their relative sizes indicating how much of the adjustment in prices occurs in the intermediate and the short runs, respectively.

$C\dot{M}H_t$ is the one-quarter rate of change in compensation per manhour. Interpreting the standard imposed lags denoted by the bars over it and $\dot{W}_t$ as indicators of the long run, $(\overline{\dot{W}}_t - \overline{C\dot{M}H}_t)$ thus measures the divergence between the long run rates of change in the fixed weight gross wage index for production workers and compensation per manhour. To the extent that the rate of growth in total labor costs exceeds the rate of growth in the fixed weight gross wage index, the two unit labor costs variables in Equation (3.2) described above understate the upward pressure increases in total labor costs place on prices. $(\overline{\dot{W}}_t - \overline{C\dot{M}H}_t)$ fills this void, as does $(\dot{W}/CMH)'_t$ in the DLA model. Its coefficient l *is expected to be negative.*

$(UFK_t - UFK_{t-1})'$ is equal to the one-quarter change in the ratio of real unfilled orders to capacity in manufacturing or zero, whichever is algebraically larger. It is used as a measure of excess demand in the private, nonfarm economy to reflect the additional upward pressure that increased excess demand in product markets places on prices, as sellers raise their markups of prices over costs in response to their improved position vis-a-vis buyers and anticipations of higher costs owing to expanding production. The asymmetric zero impact is imposed for decreases in excess demand to build into the model the downward stickiness of prices observed in the U.S. economy. Since product prices vary with markups which in turn vary directly with the degree of excess demand, m is expected to be positive.

Empirical Estimates of the ILA Equations

As we have noted, Equations (3.1) and (3.2) form a simultaneous system owing to the interdependence of wages and prices in both equations. Nevertheless, for the reasons explained in the introductory chapter we have estimated these ILA equations with OLS regression techniques.

The Wage Equation

Our estimate of the ILA wage equation for the historical period 1955:1 to 1971:2, with t-statistics in parentheses, is

$$\dot{W}_t = 0.0034 + 0.0003 \left(\frac{1}{U}\right)_t + 0.1313\,\overline{\dot{PCD}}_t + 0.1725\,\dot{JP}_t + 0.0219\,\overline{\dot{T(E)}}'_t$$
$$\quad\;(2.24)\quad\;(3.84)\qquad\quad\;(0.65)\qquad\quad(3.77)\qquad\quad(2.99)$$

$$-\,0.0019\,GP_t \qquad\qquad\qquad\qquad\qquad\qquad (3.3)$$
$$(-2.61)$$

$$\overline{R}^2 = 0.676; \quad D.W. = 2.22; \quad S.E. = 0.00241$$

As the $\overline{R}^2$ indicates, Equation (3.3) explains just over two-thirds of the variation corrected for degrees of freedom in the rate at which wages changed during the period of estimation. The Durbin-Watson statistic does not reveal any serial correlation at the 5 percent confidence level. Inspection of a correlation matrix for the independent variables, reproduced in Appendix C, suggests a multicollinearity problem between $\overline{\dot{PCD}}_t$ and $\dot{JP}_t$, since they have a simple correlation coefficient of 0.80.

All coefficients in Equation (3.3) have the expected sign and are significant, except for the coefficient on $\overline{\dot{PCD}}_t$ which is insignificant. The insignificance of the coefficient on $\overline{\dot{PCD}}_t$ appears to stem solely from its multicollinearity with $\dot{JP}_t$. First, the significant impact of $\dot{JP}_t$ demonstrates the importance of price expectations. Second, replacing $\dot{JP}_t$ with an analogous variable using a lower, three percent rate of inflation over the preceding two years as the inflation severity cutoff point, instead of the $\dot{JP}_t$ five percent figure, increased the multicollinearity problem in a test regression and reduced the size and significance of the coefficient for $\overline{\dot{PCD}}_t$ relative to Equation (3.3). Third, once adjustments have been made to allow for the fact that the ILA wage equation was originally estimated by Eckstein and Brinner with overlapping four-quarter observations, the combined impacts of $\overline{\dot{PCD}}_t$ and $\dot{JP}_t$ in Equation (3.3) are about the same as in that original equation, although distributed differently across the two variables.[d]

Abstracting from the statistical significance of its coefficient, $\overline{\dot{PCD}}_t$ implies in combination with $\dot{JP}_t$ that consumer price expectations have quite different impacts on wages in "normal" and inflationary times. In "normal" times, according to the coefficient on $\overline{\dot{PCD}}_t$, only 13 percent of an increase in the rate of price inflation will be passed on to firms in the form of more rapidly rising wages as workers adjust their price expectations with a one year lag, the other 87 percent being absorbed by workers in the form of real wages growing more slowly than needed to shift all of the inflation impact onto employers. In inflationary times when prices have risen by 5 percent or more in the preceding two years, the coefficients on $\overline{\dot{PCD}}_t$ and $\dot{JP}_t$ jointly imply that 82 percent of an increase in the rate of inflation will be passed on to firms by workers within one year and a total of 151 percent within two years.[e]

The coefficient on $\overline{T(E)}'_t$, implies that workers shift onto firms within the same quarter just under 22 percent of the wage impact which an employee tax rate change has. Since firms must subsequently shift back to workers in the next three quarters 90 percent of whatever impact is initially shifted by workers to them owing to the construction of $\overline{T(E)}'_t$, as we have already noted, this means that workers succeed in shifting to firms for more than one year only 2 percent of any wage impact produced by an employee tax rate change.

---

[d]Owing to differences in the frequency of compounding, the required adjustment can only be approximated. All that needs to be done is to multiply all of the coefficients in Equation (3.3) by four. Since our variables are expressed in decimal form and the original Eckstein-Brinner ones were expressed in percentage form, however, the constant in Equation (3.3) must also be multiplied by the additional factor of 100 and the coefficient on $(1/U)_t$ by the additional factor of 10,000. For the original estimate of the ILA wage equation, see [12, p. 4].

[e]Even ignoring the impact of $\overline{\dot{PCD}}_t$ owing to its statistical insignificance, the inflation severity variable by itself still implies workers shift forward to employers more than 100 percent of the real wage impact rapid inflation has. Subtracting the 13 percent shift stemming from $\overline{\dot{PCD}}_t$, the inflation severity impacts become 69 percent after one year and 138 percent after two years.

The Price Equation

Our estimate of the ILA price equation for the 1955:1 to 1971:2 historical period, with t-statistics in parentheses, is

$$PN\dot{F}D_t = 0.0006 + 0.8867\,(\ddot{W}_{t-1} - 0.0065) + 0.3749\,(\dot{W}_t - \ddot{W}_{t-1})$$
$$\quad\quad(1.04)\quad\;(10.00)\quad\quad\quad\quad\quad\quad\quad\quad(3.94)$$

$$\quad - 0.2284\,(\ddot{Q}_{t-1} - 0.0065) - 0.1268\,(\dot{Q}_t - \ddot{Q}_{t-1})$$
$$\quad\quad(-3.25)\quad\quad\quad\quad\quad\quad(-3.63)$$

$$\quad - 0.4199\,(\ddot{W}_t - \overline{CMH}_t) + 0.0547\,(UFK_t - UFK_{t-1})' \quad\quad (3.4)$$
$$\quad\quad(-3.08)\quad\quad\quad\quad\quad(1.76)$$

$$\bar{R}^2 = 0.733;\quad D.W. = 2.28;\quad S.E. = 0.00208$$

Equation (3.4) explains just under three-fourths of the variation corrected for degrees of freedom in the rate at which prices increased in the private, nonfarm economy during the historical period. The Durbin-Watson statistic does not indicate any serial correlation problem at the 5 percent confidence level. Inspection of a simple correlation matrix computed for the independent variables reveals no multicollinearity of the explanatory variables; the matrix is reported in Appendix C.

All coefficients in Equation (3.4) have the expected signs and magnitudes, although the one on $(UFK_t - UFK_{t-1})$ is statistically significant at only the 10 percent confidence level in a two-tailed test. The coefficient on $(\ddot{W}_{t-1} - 0.0065)$ is not significantly different from one in a one-tailed test at the 5 percent confidence level, and the constant term is insignificant, indicating that prices do increase proportionately with standard unit labor costs in the long run as required to maintain a constant income share for labor. Moreover, the coefficient on $(\dot{W}_t - \ddot{W}_{t-1})$ is significantly positive, but considerably smaller than that on $(\ddot{W}_{t-1} - 0.0065)$, providing support for the hypothesis of a lagged "administered" price adjustment to wage changes in the short run.

The pattern of coefficients on $(\ddot{W}_{t-1} - 0.0065)$, $(\ddot{Q}_{t-1} - 0.0065)$, and $(\dot{Q}_t - \ddot{Q}_{t-1})$ similarly confirms the hypothesized impact of productivity changes on prices. In the long run productivity changes are constrained to have the same impact on prices as do wage changes, since both are included in the standard unit labor cost variable reflecting their equal status as elements of that variable. In the intermediate and short runs productivity increases alleviate upward pressures on labor costs and prices, with the intermediate impact larger than the short run impact overall, yet smaller on a per quarter basis, suggesting a lagged "administered" price adjustment which tapers off over time.

Comparing the intermediate and short run impacts of productivity on unit labor costs and prices in Equation (3.4) with the short run ones of wages raises certain difficulties, for the time dimensions of the productivity and wage variables are not commensurate. For the case where the rates of productivity change differ in the short and intermediate runs, summing the coefficients of $(\dot{\overline{Q}}_{t-1} - 0.0065)$ and $(\dot{Q}_t - \dot{\overline{Q}}_{t-1})$ yields 0.3552, which comes very close as the required measure to the coefficient of 0.3749 on $(\dot{W}_t - \overline{\dot{W}}_{t-1})$. For the case where the rates of productivity change are the same in the short and intermediate runs, the coefficient of 0.2284 on $(\dot{\overline{Q}}_{t-1} - .0065)$ yields the required measure. While this coefficient is smaller than that on $(\dot{W}_t - \overline{\dot{W}}_{t-1})$, the difference is not statistically significant.[f] We conclude that the impacts which wage and productivity changes have on unit labor costs and prices in Equation (3.4) over shorter spans of time are of opposite sign but approximately equal magnitude as we would expect.

Stability Tests

Table 3-1 reports the F-statistics which resulted from tests of the structural stability of Equations (3.3) and (3.4) analogous to those done for the DLA model across subsets of the 1955:1 to 1971:2 period. The wage equation is unstable when tested for the 1955:1–1965:4 and 1966:1–1971:2 subperiod but stable for other subperiods tested. The price equation is stable for all subperiods tested. Chapter 5 discusses these test results more thoroughly.

Simulation and Mathematical Solution of the ILA Model

To evaluate the performance of the ILA model in explaining the inflation experience of the 1955:1 to 1971:2 historical period requires that its wage and price equations be considered together in order to expressly allow for the interactions which occur between them. In order to do this, we have simulated the model over the historical period and solved for the Phillips curve tradeoff between unemployment and inflation implied by the model when in long run

---

[f]Our test of the significance of this difference was only an approximate one, for it was based on the assumption that the coefficients being compared were the means to two independent, normally distributed random variables even though such an assumption is not strictly warranted. However, the correlation between $(\dot{W}_t - \overline{\dot{W}}_{t-1})$ and $(\dot{Q}_t - \dot{\overline{Q}}_{t-1})$ reported in Appendix C is so low and the normal deviate of 1.3 from our test falls so short of significance at any acceptable confidence level, that we are confident a more exact and powerful test would yield similar results.

Table 3-1

F-Statistics from Tests of Equality on the ILA Wage and Price Equations across Subsets of the 1955:1 to 1971:2 Period
(with degrees of freedom in parentheses)

	Subperiods Tested		
	1955:1 to 1960:4 and 1961:1 to 1965:4	1955:1 to 1965:4 and 1966:1 to 1971:2	1955:1 to 1960:4, 1961:1 to 1965:4, and 1966:1 to 1971:2
Wage Equation (3.3)	1.21 (6,32)	2.65 (6,54)*	1.72 (12,48)
Price Equation (3.4)	0.90 (7,30)	1.35 (7,52)	1.07 (14,45)

Source: Authors' estimates.

Note: GP_t and $\dot{J}P_t$ are zero throughout the 1955:1 to 1960:4 and the 1961:1 to 1965:4 subperiods, respectively. Each must be omitted from the wage equation covering the subperiod where it is constant in order to avoid a singular cross product matrix which cannot be inverted. The omissions are ignored in the wage equation tests of equality since they are made on account of the data, not as a priori restrictions on the coefficients. For a discussion of the procedures used to compute these F-statistics, see [8], [15], and [21, pp. 192-208].

*F-statistic significant at the 5 percent confidence level, but not at the 1 percent confidence level.

equilibrium. As we noted in the previous chapter prior to presenting the DLA model simulation, the degree to which the simulation of the ILA model captures the actual behavior of wages and prices between 1955:1 and 1971:2 should provide an informal indication of how debilitating are the biases introduced into Equations (3.3) and (3.4) by our use of OLS regression techniques.

Simulation Results

As they stand, Equations (3.3) and (3.4) do not allow for the full interaction of wages and prices, since some wage and price variables are exogenous in these two equations. To close the model with respect to wages and prices all such variables must be rendered endogenous. Despite its obvious relationship to the fixed weight gross wage index, $\overline{CMH}_t$ has been left as an exogenous variable in closing the price equation, given its secondary role in that equation, for the same reasons $(\dot{W}/CMH)'_t$ was left exogenous when simulating the DLA model: it simplifies the ILA simulation and facilitates comparison of the results with those of other simulations without any apparent adverse effect on the quality of the simulation.[g] This treatment accords with the original approach taken by Eckstein and Brinner.

$\overline{P\dot{C}D}_t$, the consumer price expectations variable, appears solely as one of the Equation (3.3) exogenous variables even though it and $P\dot{N}FD_t$, the product price dependent variable of Equation (3.4), cannot diverge in the long run according to the Gordon hypothesis to that affect adopted by Eckstein and Brinner.[6] In order to render $\overline{P\dot{C}D}_t$ endogenous in the ILA model simulation, we have linked $P\dot{C}D_t$ to $P\dot{N}FD_t$ with the same fourth degree Almon distributed lag linking equation used in simulating the DLA model. Repeated here for convenience, that linking equation as estimated for the 1949:1 to 1969:4 period is

$$P\dot{C}D_t = 0.0008 + 0.8647\,P\dot{N}FD_t + 0.1122\,P\dot{N}FD_{t-1} - 0.0880\,P\dot{N}FD_{t-2}$$
$$\quad(1.08)\quad\ (12.67)\qquad\qquad(2.46)\qquad\qquad(-2.26)$$

$$\quad - 0.0430\,P\dot{N}FD_{t-3} + 0.0384\,P\dot{N}FD_{t-4} + 0.0459\,P\dot{N}FD_{t-5}$$
$$\quad\ (-1.67)\qquad\qquad(1.10)\qquad\qquad(1.58)$$

$$\quad - 0.0322\,P\dot{N}FD_{t-6} - 0.1092\,P\dot{N}FD_{t-7}\ . \tag{2.6}$$
$$\quad\ (-1.17)\qquad\qquad(-2.62)$$

$$\overline{R}^2 = 0.738;\ \ D.W. = 1.76;\ \ S.E. = 0.00297$$

In their original study of the ILA model, Eckstein and Brinner used a distributed lag equation linking $P\dot{C}D_t$ to $P\dot{N}FD_t$ comparable to Equation (2.6) but of slightly different specification.[h] We have opted for Equation (2.6), instead of that original Eckstein and Brinner linking equation, in order to maintain consistency among our own simulation results obtained with the three different models we employ.

Figure 3-2 shows the one-quarter rates of change in wages and product prices on a quarterly basis as they actually occurred during the 1955:1 to 1971:2 period and as simulated by the ILA model. Table 3-2 reports several error measures for the simulation. The light lines in Figure 3-3 relate the changes in product prices to the unemployment rate on an annual basis for actual movements and as simulated.

The simulated wage and price changes generally, though not consistently, underpredict the actual changes, as Figure 3-2 and the positive mean errors in

---

[g]For an elaboration of this point, see footnote k in Chapter 2.

[h]Eckstein and Brinner used a second degree Almon lag extending five quarters into the past and estimated it only for the period beginning with 1955. They found the sum of the distributed lag coefficients to sum to one. See [12, p. 28]. Replicating the Ecksteing and Brinner linking equation, we also found the sum of the lag coefficients, while less than one, to differ from it by an insignificant amount at the 5 percent confidence level. See our discussion of the same point in footnote l of Chapter 2.

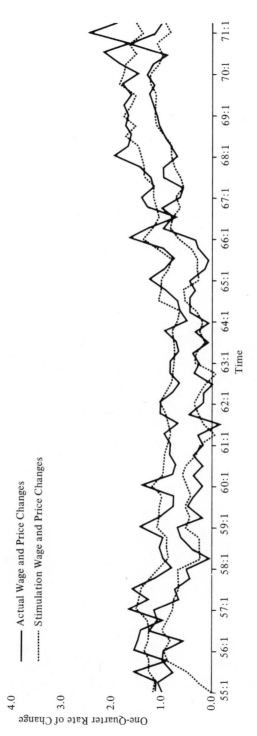

Figure 3-2. 1955:1 to 1971:2 Wage and Price Changes as They Actually Occurred and as Simulated with the ILA Model.

Table 3-2
Error Measures for the 1955:1 to 1971:2 ILA Model Simulation

	$\dot{w}_t$	$P\dot{N}FD_t$
Mean Error	0.000258315	0.0000772906
Root Mean Square Error	0.00243844	0.00202668
Mean Absolute Error	0.00184676	0.00167657
Theil U Statistic	0.98736	0.144987
Regression of actual on simulated values	$\dot{w}_t = -0.0012 + 1.1240\,\hat{\dot{w}}_t$ $\quad\;\;(-1.01)\quad(11.51)$ $\overline{R}^2 = 0.669$	$P\dot{N}FD_t = -0.0002 + 1.0533\,P\hat{\dot{N}}FD_t$ $\qquad\quad(-0.46)\quad(13.71)$ $\overline{R}^2 = 0.742$

Source: Authors' estimates.

Note: The mean of $\dot{w}_t$ is 0.0119209; the mean of $P\dot{N}FD_t$ is 0.0059960. For a description of the error measures formulae, see the note to Table 2-3.

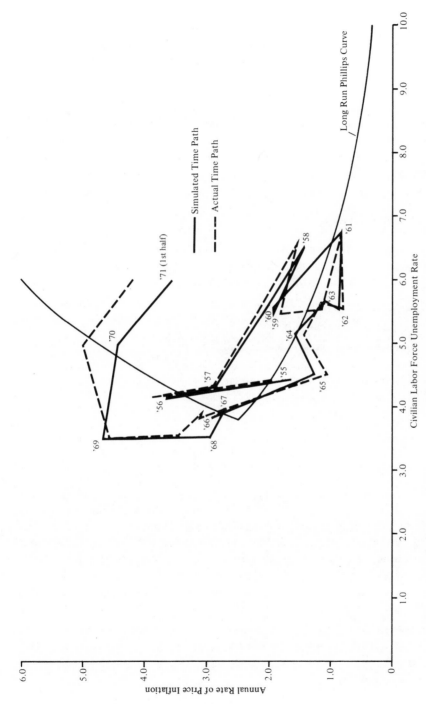

Figure 3-3. Long Run Phillips Curve and Simulated Time Path of the Economy for the ILA Model.

Table 3-2 attest. The simulation picks up turning points in wage and price changes rather well, however, and the errors do not cumulate over time. This can perhaps best be seen from the light lines in Figure 3-3. Judging from the smaller error for prices obtained with all the error measures, the simulation seems to be slightly more accurate with respect to price behavior than with respect to wage behavior. The regressions of the actual rates of change in wages and prices on the simulated rates of change in them yield intercepts not significantly different from zero and coefficients on the independent variables not significantly different from one as deterministic simulations should.[7] No serious bias problems introduced by estimating the ILA model with OLS regressions are obvious.

Long Run Phillips Curve

Solving Equation (3.3) and (3.4) simultaneously under appropriate steady state assumptions yields the long run Phillips curve implied by the ILA model. Our solution is based on the following assumptions:

1. all prices change in the same proportion;
2. tax rates are constant;
3. product market excess demand conditions are constant;
4. compensation per manhour grows in the long run at a quarterly rate exceeding by 0.005 percentage points the corresponding rate of growth in the fixed weight gross wage index;
5. there are no wage-price guideposts in effect; and
6. wages, prices, and productivity have been growing at their constant, steady state rates long enough for intitial conditions and lag structures to have no impacts.[i]

The heavy kinked line in Figure 3-3 traces out the long run ILA model unemployment-inflation tradeoff corresponding to our assumptions. As it shows, the long run Phillips curve is composed of two distinct segments. In "normal" times when inflation has occurred at an average rate of 2.5 percent per annum or less during the previous two year period the Phillips curve has the usual negative

---

[i]The fourth assumption regarding the rates of change in compensation per manhour and the fixed weight gross wage index is taken directly from Gordon's original analysis of the DLA model and corresponds to the fourth assumption made when solving for the long run Phillips curve of that model in the preceding chapter. See [18, p. 136] and footnote m in Chapter 2. Taking account of the fact that Gordon used $(C\dot{M}H/W)_t$ while we use $(\bar{\dot{W}}_t - \overline{\dot{CMH}}_t)$, leads to a small compounding and rounding error we have ignored and the sign reversal we have made.

slope. When inflation has occurred at an average rate in excess of 2.5 percent per annum over those two years, however, explosive price expectations form, the inflation severity variable $\dot{JP}_t$ becomes positive, and the Phillips curve takes on a positive slope reflecting the potential for explosive inflation cumulating throughout the economy.

The steady state tradeoffs between unemployment and inflation implied by the ILA model are stable in the "normal" range where the Phillips curve has a negative slope. They are unstable above the 2.5 percent level of inflation where the curve takes on a positive slope, however. As with the DLA model, a perturbation of the economy while in such a steady state would lead to a cumulating inflation or deflation. Here, however, a deflation would not continue indefinitely, because the rate of inflation would decline only until the stable portion of the Phillips curve were reached.

Under our assumptions, the original Eckstein-Brinner version of the Phillips curve also has a positively sloped portion even though Eckstein and Brinner drew it as a vertical line.[8] They may well have drawn this portion of the curve in a manner consistent with the acceleration hypothesis owing to the steady state instability we have found.

Each annual unemployment-inflation experience depicted by the light line time paths in Figure 3-3 can be thought of as lying on a short run Phillips curve, flatter in slope than the long run curve, which shifts position over time.

4

A Current Period Adjustment Model

The current period adjustment (henceforth CPA) model described in this chapter is a modified version of an inflation model originally developed for the manufacturing sector by Calvin Siebert and Mahmood Zaidi in a previous study.[1] Both as originally specified and as employed here, it differs from the DLA and ILA models already presented substantially more than they differ between themselves.

Siebert and Zaidi's expressed purpose was not so much to explain the inflation process, as to test several specific hypotheses related to the separate determination of wages and prices per se in manufacturing. They specified a general model of the inflation process containing a wage equation and a price equation, but never estimated the complete equations nor examined the interactions between them. Instead, they ran regressions for 15 different subsets of the wage equation variables and 5 different subsets of the price equation variables, and then made comparisons within these two groups of regressions in order to draw inferences about the specific wage determination and price determination hypotheses of interest to them.

In order to establish our version of the CPA model for the private, nonfarm economy, we have reformulated the Siebert and Zaidi analysis in two major respects. First, we have switched from the manufacturing data base used by Siebert and Zaidi to the private, nonfarm sector one used for the DLA and ILA model presentations, leaving the construction procedures for the actual CPA model variables based on this new data unchanged from those specified by Siebert and Zaidi whenever feasible. Second, we have replicated the regressions actually run by Siebert and Zaidi, tested a few additional variants of such regressions not considered by them, and estimated the complete wage and price equations only specified by them in order to ascertain which versions of the wage and price equations perform best for the private, nonfarm economy. Appendix D summarizes the results for this second stage of our analysis. As the final version of the CPA model for the private, nonfarm economy we have adopted with one modification the wage equation and the price equation in Appendix D having the highest $\overline{R}^2$'s of all those tried.[a]

---

[a]The Appendix D wage equations use the current dollar amount of profits as the profits variable. In the final version of the CPA model we shifted to the rate of change in profits. Our reasons for making the modification are elaborated upon later in this chapter. Our estimates of the final version of the CPA model presented in this chapter are based on data revised since the Appendix D equations were estimated.

Specification of the CPA Model

The current period adjustment model we have adopted for presentation here contains a wage equation and a price equation which form a simultaneous system, since prices are explicitly introduced into the wage equation and vice-versa. Despite the name given to the model, not all adjustments take place in the current period. The price equation contains no lags, but the wage equation does. Complete definitions of all variables and descriptions of all data sources are provided in Appendixes A and B, respectively.

The Wage Equation

The CPA wage equation is eclectic in the same sense as are those of the DLA and ILA models, for it contains variables designed to capture a variety of influences.[b] However, it includes certain variables not contained in either of the other two wage equations and omits the tax variables appearing in both of them. The equation to be fitted is

$$\dot{W}_t = a + b\left(\frac{1}{U}\right)_t + c\,\dot{U}_t + d\,\dot{PCD}_t + e\,\dot{PNFD}_t + f\,\dot{Q}_t + g\,\dot{C}_t + h\,\dot{W}_{t-1}, \quad (4.1)$$

where the t subscripts refer to quarter-year time periods and dots above variables indicate their use in rate of change form.

$\dot{W}_t$, the dependent variable of the wage equation, is the one-quarter rate of change in the fixed weight gross wage index used in the DLA and ILA models. It includes fringe benefits and is adjusted for manufacturing overtime and interindustry employment shifts. It covers production workers in the private, nonfarm economy.

$(1/U)_t$ is the reciprocal of the civilian labor force unemployment rate, with that rate expressed in decimal form. It is used to represent excess supply in the labor market, which in turn is a measure of labor market tightness and the bargaining power of the parties involved. When the excess supply of labor is small, the labor market is tight, workers have a strong bargaining position relative to firms seeking to hire them, and upward pressures on wages increase as a result. Since it varies inversely with the excess supply of labor, the reciprocal of the unemployment rate varies directly with the extent of any upward pressure put on wages by labor market conditions. Therefore, b is expected to be positive.

---

[b]Since Siebert and Zaidi wanted to test a number of competing hypotheses, they included in the general formulation of their wage equation variables representing all these hypotheses. Our final version CPA wage equation turned out eclectic only because in our Appendix D analysis this generalized wage equation outperformed the hypothesis-specific wage equations actually estimated by Siebert and Zaidi.

$\dot{U}_t$ is the one-quarter rate of change in the civilian labor force unemployment rate. Siebert and Zaidi interpreted it as an expectational variable.[2] In our own view such an approach is unnecessarily narrow. We prefer to consider $\dot{U}_t$ a measure of the hysteresis loop effects Phillips found in his analysis of the curve named for him.[3] According to this interpretation, a falling unemployment rate leads to faster wage growth for two reasons. First, a falling unemployment rate is generally associated with net hiring of workers, which leads firms to offer better wages than they otherwise would in order to attract the additional workers desired.[c] Second, a falling unemployment rate generates expectations of a tighter labor market in the future, prompting employers to hire unnecessary workers and bid more for labor than they ordinarily would in the present, so as to avoid hiring and bargaining in the future, when wages and unit labor costs are expected to be higher. We presume Siebert and Zaidi had this second effect in mind when terming $\dot{U}_t$ an expectational variable even though they never said so explicitly. Reflecting the upward pressure which a falling unemployment rate places on wages via both impacts described, c is expected to be negative.

$\dot{PCD}_t$ is the one-quarter rate of change in the GNP implicit price deflator for personal consumption expenditures. It is used by Siebert and Zaidi to capture the impact consumer price changes have on the rate of growth in money wages by affecting real wages and thereby altering workers' bargaining stance. Alternatively, it can be viewed as a measure of price expectations just as it is in the DLA and ILA models. Ignoring for the moment the presence of $\dot{W}_{t-1}$ in Equation (4.1) as a lagged endogenous variable, the only difference is that here there is no lag in the extrapolation of past experience into future expectations. On the one hand, this implies a willingness to rapidly adjust expectations to current experience; on the other hand, it means a myopic inability to recall the lessons of the past. In recognition of the extra incentive workers have to put upward pressure on wages by bargaining for large higher money wage increases when consumer prices are rising, d is expected to be positive. Owing to the fact that the impact of higher consumer prices on wages is restricted to an average, constant percentage pass-through as in the DLA model, rather than distinguishing between the negligible impacts of small consumer price changes workers frequently ignore versus the substantial impacts of large consumer price changes they try to pass on completely with 100 percent forward shifting as in the ILA model, d is expected to be less than one.

$\dot{PNFD}_t$ is the one-quarter rate of change in the GNP implicit price deflator for the private, nonfarm economy. Siebert and Zaidi used it as one element of the

---

[c]The general case need not necessarily hold, however. A falling unemployment rate could also be associated with a net firing of workers if the labor force were declining rapidly enough. Conversely, a rising unemployment rate could be associated with a net hiring of workers if the labor force were growing rapidly enough. Indeed, the Nixon Administration claimed this latter situation existed during much of 1970 and 1971. See [44, pp. 67] and [45].

rate of change in value productivity.[d] Equivalently, it can be viewed as a product price variable analogous to $(P\dot{N}FD-P\dot{C}D)_t$ in the DLA model. In either case, it is designed to capture the impact which product prices have on wages by affecting the demand for labor. Since it renders the output of labor more valuable, an increase in product prices increases the demand for labor and puts added upward pressure on wages by tightening the labor market. In reflection of this pattern, e is expected to be positive.

$\dot{Q}_t$ is the one-quarter rate of change in output per manhour in the private, nonfarm sector. It is used to capture the effects which changes in labor productivity have on wages. So long as wages and labor productivity change in the same proportion, unit labor costs are not affected.[e] Consequently, workers' ability to bargain for higher wages should vary with the rate of growth in their productivity. The coefficient f is expected to be positive as a consequence of this relationship. Since most workers are able to renegotiate their wages only at specific points in time, not continuously, and the specification of $\dot{Q}_t$ in Equation (4.1) makes no provision for a lag in the adjustment of wages following productivity gains, f is expected to capture only the partial wage adjustment that occurs immediately following productivity change. This suggests a value for f less than one.

$\dot{C}_t$ is the one-quarter rate of change in current dollar corporate profits before tax. It is used as a proxy for the profit rate of all firms to reflect the impact profitability has on the relative bargaining position of workers and firms, but may also capture some product markets demand effects since profits fluctuate with the level of economic activity. Precisely what profit rate variable Siebert and Zaidi used in their original study is unknown to us. After finding the dollar amount of corporate profits to have virtually no impact in our preliminary analysis summarized in Appendix D, we adopted $\dot{C}_t$ as our profit rate variable owing to its computational simplicity in spite of some limitations of it as a measure of the level of profitability.[f] Inasmuch as higher profits make firms susceptible to worker demand for sharing in the success of the firm via higher wages, g is expected to be positive.

---

[d]Siebert and Zaidi used the rate of change in the wholesale price index for manufacturing as their price variable. We have replaced it with $PNFD_t$ in shifting the analysis from the manufacturing sector to the entire private, nonfarm economy. The rate of change in value productivity is equal to the sum of the rates of change in product prices and productivity. This definition of the relationship between average value productivity and product price is presented in Equation (2) in [42, p. 280].

[e]If the quantity of output produced with one unit of labor increases by x percent, the wage paid to that unit of labor can rise up to x percent without causing the unit labor cost of the output of increase.

[f]The difficulties with $\dot{C}_t$ as a measure of the level of profitability stem from the fact that it

$\dot{W}_{t-1}$ is simply the dependent variable of Equation (4.1) lagged one period. Its inclusion as an explanatory variable is equivalent to imposing a Koyck distributed lag on all the other explanatory variables, of course, but this was not the intention of Siebert and Zaidi. Rather, they introduced the lag to recognize the fact that wage contracts expire at discrete time intervals, cannot be renegotiated immediately and continuously every time conditions affecting wages change, and take months to spill over among industries. Recognizing the impossibility of empirically distinguishing between this interpretation and the Koyck lag one, we nevertheless wish to stress this latter interpretation of $\dot{W}_{t-1}$ for two reasons.[4] First, including $\dot{W}_{t-1}$ in the wage equation adds little to the explanatory power of that equation and leaves the coefficients on the other wage equation explanatory variables relatively undisturbed as compared with their values for the case where it is left out, as can be seen from the results presented in Appendix D. Second, the coefficient on $\dot{W}_{t-1}$ in Equation (4.3) implies Koyck lag impacts of the other explanatory variables that diminish rapidly compared to the lag impacts estimated with the DLA and ILA models. Regardless of which interpretation is given to $\dot{W}_{t-1}$, however, its appearance in Equation (4.1) means the CPA model is not a current period adjustment model in the true sense even though relative to the DLA and ILA models it does adjust quickly. Since the forces which lead to a partial adjustment of wages in the first period should lead them to adjust in the same direction with a lag in subsequent periods, h is expected to be positive.

The Price Equation

Unlike the DLA and ILA price equations, the CPA price equation is not based on the hypothesis that wages are the only driving force behind prices in the long run and constitute a constant share of income. For, it explicitly recognizes materials costs as a major determinant of prices. Nor does the CPA price equation attempt to distinguish between the long and short run impacts various

---

measures the rate of change in the level of profits as opposed to the level itself. If workers bargain for wage increases on the basis of how fast profits rise, then $\dot{C}_t$ is an appropriate form of the profit variable. However, if workers bargain on the basis of the level of profits, whether in absolute terms, relative to the amount of capital or equity invested, or relative to sales, without regard to how fast profits have been growing and are expected to grow in the near future, then $\dot{C}_t$ is inappropriate. That we found $\dot{C}_t$ insignificant in the Appendix D regressions does not demonstrate that profits are unimportant, because the strong secular trend in $\dot{C}_t$ creates problems in testing for a longitudinal impact of profitability on wages. As an illustration of a preferable variable, see Perry's work using the ratio of profits to equity, which he found to have a significant impact on wages, in [33, pp. 292-293] and [34, pp. 48-49].

factors have on prices. No lags of any kind appear in the CPA price equation; it is a current adjustment not only relative to the DLA and ILA price equations, but also in the absolute sense.

The CPA price equation to be fitted is

$$P\dot{N}FD_t = i + j\,\dot{W}_t + k\,\dot{Q}_t + l\,R\dot{M}P_t + m\,C\dot{U}R_t + n\left(\frac{UF_t - UF_{t-1}}{S_t}\right), \quad (4.2)$$

where the t subscripts refer to quarter-year time periods and dots above variables indicate their use in rate of change form as before.

The dependent variable of Equation (4.2), $P\dot{N}FD_t$, should need no explanation by now. It is the same product price variable, namely the one-quarter rate of change in the GNP implicit price deflator for the private, nonfarm economy, appearing in the CPA wage equation and in both of the other two models already presented.

$\dot{W}_t$ is the one-quarter rate of change in the fixed weight gross wage index employed as the dependent variable of the CPA wage equation. It is utilized in the price equation to measure the impact wages have on prices as a major element of unit costs. No attempt is made to distinguish standard costs from actual ones. The coefficient j is expected to be positive, because an increase in wages increases unit costs and places upward pressure on prices. Since other major elements of cost are also included in Equation (4.2), and no attempt is made to measure total, long run impacts through the use of lags, there is no reason why j should not be less than one. However, the constant term i is nevertheless expected to diverge only insignificantly from zero as a reflection of the fact that prices vary directly with total unit costs.

$\dot{Q}_t$ is the one-quarter rate of change in output per manhour as in wage Equation (4.1). It measures the other half of unit labor cost changes not picked up by $\dot{W}_t$. Since productivity increases offset wage and other cost element increases and alleviate upward pressures on costs, as already noted, productivity should have a negative impact on prices at the same time it has a positive one on wages. Consequently, k is expected to be negative notwithstanding the positive impact expected for productivity in the wage equation.

$R\dot{M}P_t$ is the one-quarter rate of change in the raw industrial commodities component of the nonseasonally adjusted wholesale price index. It is utilized to catch the impact changing raw materials prices have as an element of unit costs on product prices in general. Its coefficient l is expected to be positive, because an increase in any element of unit costs should put upward pressure on prices unless offset by a commensurate decline in another element of unit costs, but less than one since raw materials account for only a portion of unit costs.

An expansion in the demand for its product can affect the price decisions of a firm in two contrasting ways in the short run. On the one hand, unit costs tend to decline as more effective use is made of factor inputs, including labor, which are of a quasifixed nature. On the other hand, its improved market position relative to purchasers of its product provides the firm with a profit maximizing incentive to raise its markup of prices over unit costs. $\dot{CUR}_t$ is the one-quarter rate of change in the Federal Reserve Board capacity utilization index for manufacturing. It is used as a proxy for the price lowering impact which an expansion of demand has by lowering unit costs. Its coefficient m is expected to be negative. $(UF_t - UF_{t-1})/S_t$ is the ratio of the one-quarter change in the current dollar ratio of the backlog of unfilled orders in manufacturing to the level of sales in manufacturing and trade. It is used to capture the price raising impact which an expansion of demand has by improving the market position of sellers relative to buyers. Its coefficient n is expected to be positive.

Empirical Estimates of the CPA Equations

Despite the fact that Equations (4.1) and (4.2) form a simultaneous system owing to the interaction of wages and prices in both equations and could more readily be estimated with simultaneous equations techniques than could the DLA and ILA equations, we have relied on OLS regression techniques in estimating these two equations for the reasons discussed in the introductory chapter just as we have in estimating the DLA and ILA equations. In the particular case of the CPA model, however, this raises potential problems of biased and inconsistent coefficient estimates independently of the simultaneity induced problems owing to the presence of the lagged dependent variable in the wage equation.[5]

The Wage Equation

Our OLS estimate of the CPA wage equation for the 1955:1 to 1971:2 historical period, with t-statistics in parentheses, is

$$\dot{W}_t = 0.0021 + 0.0001\left(\frac{1}{U}\right)_t - 0.0021\,\dot{U}_t + 0.4992\,PCD_t + 0.3202\,PN\dot{F}D_t$$
$$\phantom{\dot{W}_t =}(1.09)\quad(0.74)\qquad\quad(-0.34)\qquad(3.10)\qquad\quad(2.28)$$

$$+ 0.1070\,\dot{Q}_t + 0.0141\,\dot{C}_t + 0.2267\,\dot{W}_{t-1}$$
$$(1.98)\qquad(1.54)\qquad(2.21)$$

$$\overline{R}^2 = 0.663;\quad D.W. = 2.13;\quad S.E. = 0.00245 \qquad\qquad (4.3)$$

Equation (4.3) explains almost exactly two-thirds of the variation corrected for degrees of freedom that occurred in the rate of wage change during the historical period of estimation, as the $\overline{R}^2$ shows. The Durbin-Watson statistic falls far short of significance at the 5 percent confidence level, but cannot be accepted as firm evidence of no serial correlation, because the appearance of the lagged dependent variable biases it in the direction of accepting the null hypothesis. Computation of the h-statistic developed by Durbin for large sample tests of serial correlation with equations containing lagged dependent variables also results in acceptance of the null hypothesis, however, confirming the tentative conclusion drawn from the Durbin-Watson statistic.[g] This finding is significant, because it indicates that consistency problems are not introduced into Equation (4.3) by the presence of the lagged dependent variable even though bias problems still arise in connection with the finite sample size.[6]

All of the variable coefficients in Equation (4.3) are of the expected sign, but a surprising number are statistically insignificant in two-tailed tests at the 5 percent confidence level. At least part of the explanation for this insignificance appears related to multicollinearity among the independent variables. Inspection of a correlation matrix for the independent variables, reproduced in Appendix C, indicates a high degree of multicollinearity among $P\dot{C}D_t$, $P\dot{N}FD_t$, and $\dot{W}_{t-1}$ and between $\dot{Q}_t$ and $\dot{C}_t$.

$P\dot{C}D_t$ and $P\dot{N}FD_t$ both have significant impacts in Equation (4.3) despite being multicollinear with respect to each other and $\dot{W}_{t-1}$. The coefficient on $P\dot{C}D_t$ suggests that during the same quarter workers pass on to their employers in the form of wage increases about 50 percent of any increase in consumer prices. The coefficient on $P\dot{N}FD_t$ implies that employers also absorb another 32 percent of product price increases in the same quarter as a result of increases in the demand for labor stemming from the higher product prices. Together the two coefficients indicate that employers pay for approximately 82 percent of a general price inflation in the form of higher money wages, while workers pay for about 18 percent in the form of lower real wages. On the one hand, this 82 percent pass-through is considerably higher than that implied by either the DLA or ILA model in so short a period. On the other hand, it is smaller than that generally implied by the other two models in the long run.[h] The discrepancy can be traced to the presence of lags on $P\dot{C}D_t$ and $P\dot{N}FD_t$ which cause the short and long run impacts to differ in the other two models and their absence which causes these impacts to be the same in the CPA model.

---

[g]The Durbin h-statistic for Equation (4.3) is 0.204. Since h is a standard normal deviate, it would have to be 1.64 or larger to be significant at even the 10 percent confidence level. See [11], [21, pp. 307-313], and [31].

[h]Setting $\dot{W}_t = \dot{W}_{t-1}$, the long run pass-through becomes 106 percent. This is less than the long run pass-through implied by the DLA model and the ILA model in inflationary periods, but more than that implied by the ILA model under "normal" circumstances.

We are unable to offer a convincing explanation for the insignificance of the unemployment variables in Equation (4.3). $(1/U)_t$ has the same, insignificant impact in a modified CPA wage equation even when $\dot{U}_t$ is suppressed, for example, which is a marked contrast to its significance when it appears as the only measure of labor market tightness in the DLA and ILA wage equations. One possibility, for which we have no supporting evidence, is that the omission of a price expectations lag from the CPA wage equation forces the unemployment inverse to pick up the offsetting impacts high unemployment and inflationary expectations had in the late 1960s, as opposed to just the former impacts, thereby limiting the net effectiveness of the variable as a determinant of wages.[i]

Edwin Kuh has argued that profits serve as a proxy for productivity in a wage equation, since profits are high when productivity is high, and should be replaced by productivity itself.[7] Such a view provides one explanation for both the multicollinearity between $\dot{Q}_t$ and $\dot{C}_t$ and the insignificance of $\dot{C}_t$ in Equation (4.3). An alternative explanation for this unimportance of $\dot{C}_t$ lies in our use of the profits rate of change variable instead of a profit level variable, a point already touched upon in explaining the CPA wage equation specification. Profits expressed as a rate of return might well have a significant impact on wages separate from, if similar to, the impact productivity has, even though the change in that profit rate has no impact in Equation (4.3). To distinguish between these two interpretations would require specifying and testing a profit level variable with the secular trend eliminated from it, an exercise peripheral to our main avenue of inquiry with the CPA model.

The Price Equation

Our estimate of the CPA price equation for the 1955:1 to 1971:2 historical period, with t-statistics in parentheses, is

$$PN\dot{F}D_t = -0.0011 + 0.6623\,\dot{W}_t - 0.1534\,\dot{Q}_t - 0.0024\,R\dot{M}P_t$$
$$\quad (-1.16) \quad (9.27) \qquad (-3.28) \qquad (-0.22)$$

$$-0.0248\,C\dot{U}R_t + 0.0694\left(\frac{UF_t - UF_{t-1}}{S_t}\right).$$
$$\quad (-1.32) \qquad (2.08)$$

$$\bar{R}^2 = 0.639; \quad D.W. = 1.93; \quad S.E. = 0.00242$$

(4.4)

---

[i]When $\dot{U}_t$ is suppressed, the CPA wage equation $\bar{R}^2$ remains virtually unchanged, rising 0.005 to 0.668, and the coefficient on $(1/U)_t$ remains unchanged at 0.0001, its t-coefficient rising to 1.08. Labor market changes and price expectations have already been

It explains 64 percent of the variation corrected for degrees of freedom in the rate at which prices rose during the period of estimation. The Durbin-Watson statistic reveals no serial correlation at the 5 percent confidence level. Inspection of a correlation matrix prepared for the independent variables, and contained in Appendix C, shows that there is a minor multicollinearity problem stemming from the positive correlation of $C\dot{U}R_t$ with both $\dot{Q}_t$ and $(UF_t - UF_{t-1})/S_t)$, which are not correlated themselves, but no major multicollinearity problems are evident from such an inspection.

All coefficients have the expected sign and are statistically significant at the 5 percent confidence level in two-tailed tests, except for the intercept term which is insignificant as expected, $R\dot{M}P_t$, and $C\dot{U}R_t$. The coefficient on $\dot{W}_t$ is significantly positive as expected, and also significantly less than one as we suggested it might be. According to Equation (4.4), about two-thirds of the impact which an increase in wages has on unit costs is passed on as a price increase in the same quarter. This is a considerably faster reaction than that implied by either the DLA or ILA price equation, reflecting to a large extent the fact that subsequent adjustments are not allowed for in the specification of Equation (4.4), as they are in the specifications of the DLA and ILA price equations which separate long from short run impacts.

The insignificance of $R\dot{M}P_t$ in Equation (4.4) is at first surprising, for it seems to contradict the "cost plus" markup hypothesis that forms a key cog in the theory of "administered" prices. However, there are at least two explanations for this result. First, Equation (4.4) covers the entire private, nonfarm economy, for parts of which raw materials prices have very little impact on the prices charged to customers. The insignificance of raw material prices for these parts of the economy could lead to the insignificance of $R\dot{M}P_t$ in Equation (4.4) whether or not raw material prices were important in other parts of the economy. Second, the raw industrial commodities component of the wholesale price index we have used in constructing $R\dot{M}P_t$ is not a good measure of raw material input prices. It is not seasonally adjusted, for instance, while all other data series used to construct the variable appearing in Equation (4.4) are. We have used this particular data series in spite of misgivings about it for lack of a better series, not because we thought it an ideal measure of the influence we sought to represent.

The insignificance of $C\dot{U}R_t$ must be at least partially attributed to the multicollinearity between it and both $\dot{Q}_t$ and $(UF_t - UF_{t-1})/S_t$. Such multicollinearity should hardly be surprising, for productivity, capacity utilization, and order backlogs all change in concert as the level of economic activity changes. Whether the coefficient on $C\dot{U}R_t$ is insignificant because the data are

---

discussed as alternative explanations for the 1955:1 to 1971:2 inflation experience in connection with the DLA model. See Chapter 2 and the references cited in bibliographical note 5 to that chapter.

not fine enough to distinguish among the effects of the three variables or because $C\dot{U}R_t$ simply has no independent effect cannot be determined from Equation (4.4).

Stability Tests

Table 4-1 reports the F-statistics from tests on the structural stability of Equations (4.3) and (4.4) across subsets of the 1955:1 to 1971:2 period. The wage equation was stable for all periods tested. The price equation was unstable when tested for the 1955:1 to 1965:4 and 1966:1 to 1971:2 subperiods, but stable otherwise. Chapter 5 treats these test results at greater length.

Simulation and Mathematical Solution of the CPA Model

As with the DLA and ILA models, the equations of the CPA model form a simultaneous system whose interactions require that the model be examined in its entirety, not equation by equation, in order to determine how well it tracks the inflation experience of the 1955:1 to 1971:2 historical period. Consequently, once again, we have both simulated the model over the historical period and solved for the Phillips curve tradeoff between unemployment and inflation implied by the model when in long run equilibrium . How well the CPA model simulation captures the actual behavior of wages and prices during the 1955:1 to 1971:2 period should provide some informal indication of whether the

Table 4-1
F-Statistics from Tests of Equality on the CPA Wage and Price Equations across Subsets of the 1955:1 to 1971:2 Period
(with degress of freedom in parentheses)

	Subperiods Tested		
	1955:1 to 1960:4 and 1961:1 to 1965:4	*1955:1 to 1965:4 and 1966:1 to 1971:2*	*1955:1 to 1960:4, 1961:1 to 1965:4, and 1966:1 to 1971:2*
Wage Equation (4.3)	1.18 (8,28)	1.63 (8,50)	1.28 (16,42)
Price Equation (4.4)	0.92 (6,32)	2.75 (6,54)*	1.80 (12,48)

Source: Authors' estimates.

Note: For a discussion of the procedures used to compute these F-statistics, see [8], [15], and [21, pp. 192-208].

*F-statistic significant at the 5 percent confidence level, but not at the 1 percent confidence level.

simultaneity and lagged dependent variables biases introduced into Equations (4.3) and (4.4) by our reliance on OLS estimation procedures seriously compromise the predictive power of the CPA model.

Simulation Results

Equations (4.3) and (4.4) are inappropriate by themselves for a full simulation of the 1955:1 to 1971:2 inflation experience, because they do not allow for the full dynamic interaction of wages and prices. Wages are completely endogenous within the CPA model, since no compensation per manhour variable appears as a cost supplement to wages in the price equation, but two of the price variables are not endogenous. Consequently, we have transformed $P\dot{C}D_t$ and $R\dot{M}P_t$ into endogenous variables for simulation purposes by linking them to previous values of $PN\dot{F}D_t$.

For $P\dot{C}D_t$ we have used the same fourth degree Almon distributed lag equation utilized in the DLA and ILA model simulations. Repeated here for convenience with t-statistics in parentheses, that linking equation estimated for the 1949:1 to 1969:1 period is

$$P\dot{C}D_t = 0.0008 + 0.8647\,PN\dot{F}D_t + 0.1122\,PN\dot{F}D_{t-1} - 0.0880\,PN\dot{F}D_{t-2}$$
$$\phantom{P\dot{C}D_t =} (1.08) \quad (12.67) \qquad\quad (2.46) \qquad\qquad\quad (-2.26)$$

$$- 0.0430\,PN\dot{F}D_{t-3} + 0.0384\,PN\dot{F}D_{t-4} + 0.0459\,PN\dot{F}D_{t-5}$$
$$(-1.67) \qquad\qquad (1.10) \qquad\qquad\quad (1.58)$$

$$- 0.0322\,PN\dot{F}D_{t-6} - 0.1092\,PN\dot{F}D_{t-7}\,. \tag{2.6}$$
$$(-1.17) \qquad\qquad (-2.62)$$

$$\bar{R}^2 = 0.738; \quad \text{D.W.} = 1.76; \quad \text{S.E.} = 0.00297$$

For $R\dot{M}P_t$ we have estimated another, new equation exactly analogous to Equation (2.6) with respect to both the lag structure and period of estimation. The theoretical justification for such an equation is much weaker in the case of $R\dot{M}P_t$ than in the case of $P\dot{C}D_t$ for two reasons, however. First, $R\dot{M}P_t$ is much more likely to lead $PN\dot{F}D_t$ or move independently of it than to lag it and be determined by it as $P\dot{C}D_t$ is in the long run. Second, the fact that $R\dot{M}P_t$ is not seasonally adjusted and $PN\dot{F}D_t$ is introduces additional noise into, and reduces the explanatory power of, any equation linking the two variables. We have linked $R\dot{M}P_t$ to $PN\dot{F}D_t$ despite these problems for lack of any clearly superior alternative of comparable simplicity. The $R\dot{M}P_t$ equation, estimated for the 1949:1 to 1969:4 period, with t-statistics in parentheses, is

$$\dot{RMP}_t = 0.0215 + 5.8977\,\dot{PNFD}_t - 0.7133\,\dot{PNFD}_{t-1} - 2.8584\,\dot{PNFD}_{t-2}$$
$$\quad(2.02)\quad(6.07)\qquad\quad(-1.08)\qquad\qquad(-5.07)$$

$$\qquad - 2.6526\,\dot{PNFD}_{t-3} - 1.6337\,\dot{PNFD}_{t-4} - 0.7630\,\dot{PNFD}_{t-5}$$
$$\qquad\quad(-7.11)\qquad\qquad(-3.24)\qquad\qquad(-1.81)$$

$$\qquad - 0.4249\,\dot{PNFD}_{t-6} - 0.4269\,\dot{PNFD}_{t-7}\,. \qquad\qquad\qquad (4.5)$$
$$\qquad\quad(-1.07)\qquad\qquad(-0.71)$$

$$\bar{R}^2 = 0.516;\quad \text{D.W.} = 1.65;\quad \text{S.E.} = 0.04298$$

The sum of the lag coefficients in Equation (4.5) is -3.5750 and significantly less than one, reflecting not only the fact that raw material prices rose more slowly than product prices in general during the 1949:1 to 1969:4 period, but also the limited theoretical justification for the equation.[j]

Figure 4-1 traces out the one-quarter rates of change in wages and product prices on a quarterly basis as they actually occurred during the 1955:1 to 1971:2 period and as simulated by the CPA model. Table 4-2 reports several error measures for the simulation. The light lines in Figure 4-2 relate the changes in product prices to the unemployment rate on an annual basis for actual and simulated movements.

As Figure 4-1 shows, the simulated values of wages and prices fluctuate erratically between underprediction and overprediction in individual quarters. This erratic fluctuation overshadows by far the average overprediction of wages and prices indicated by the positive mean errors in Table 4-2. Although the simulation picks up the majority of turning points in the rates of wage and price change, it misses too many to be termed satisfactory in this regard and understates the variability of wage and price changes over time. This can be seen quite clearly in Figure 4-2, which shows that the simulated wage and price changes frequently bear little relation to the actual ones. The regressions of the actual rates of change in wages and prices on the simulated rates of change suggest that serious biases may have emerged in this regard, from our estimation of the CPA model with OLS techniques, for the intercept term is significantly positive, and the independent variable coefficient is significantly less than unity for both the wage and price change regressions.

Long Run Phillips Curve

Simultaneous solution of Equations (4.3) and (4.4) under appropriate steady

---

[j]Preliminary simulations of the CPA model with $\dot{RMP}_t$ left exogenous did not work as well as ones with it rendered endogenous, notwithstanding the poor fit of Equation (4.5). This probably reflects the insignificance of $\dot{RMP}_t$ in the price equation and the reduction of noise achieved by rendering it endogenous more than it reflects the success of our CPA model

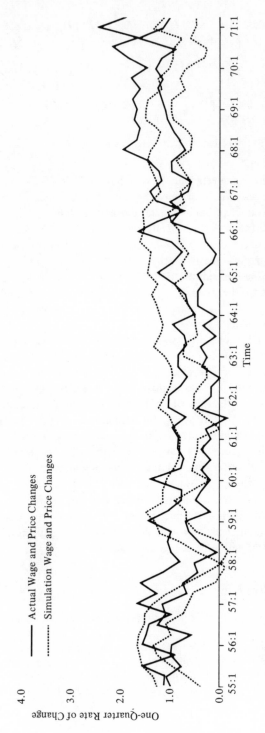

Figure 4-1. 1955:1 to 1971:2 Wage and Price Changes as They Actually Occurred and as Simulated with the CPA Model.

Table 4-2
Error Measures for the 1955:1 to 1971:2 CPA Model Simulation

	$\dot{w}_t$	$P\dot{N}FD_t$
Mean Error	0.0000943516	0.0000599409
Root Mean Square Error	0.00473728	0.00385734
Mean Absolute Error	0.00379961	0.00324394
Theil U Statistics	0.190584	0.278991
Regression of actual on simulated values	$\dot{w}_t = 0.0090 + 0.2442\,\hat{\dot{w}}_t$ $\quad\ \ (4.40)\quad\ (1.45)$ $\overline{R}^2 = 0.017$	$P\dot{N}FD_t = 0.0026 + 0.5677\,P\hat{\dot{N}}FD_t$ $\qquad\qquad (2.55)\quad\ (3.64)$ $\overline{R}^2 = 0.159$

Source: Authors' estimates.

Note: The mean of $\dot{w}_t$ is 0.0119209; the mean of $P\dot{N}FD_t$ is 0.0059960. For a description of the error measures formulae, see the note to Table 2-3.

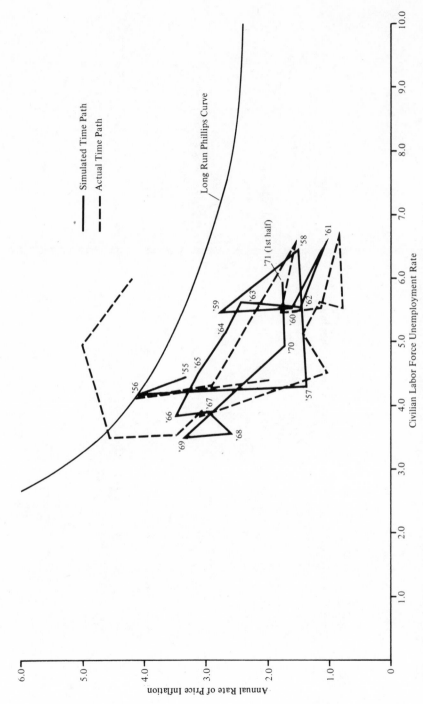

Figure 4-2. Long Run Phillips Curve and Simulated Time Path of the Economy for the CPA Model.

state assumptions yields the long run Phillips curve consistent with the CPA model. Our solution is based on the following assumptions:

1. all prices change in the same proportion;
2. labor market excess demand conditions are constant, resulting in a constant unemployment rate;
3. product market excess demand conditions are constant, resulting in a constant unfilled orders to sales ratio;
4. productivity grows at its long run, steady state rate;
5. profits grow at their long run, steady state rate; and
6. wages have been growing at their long run, steady state rate for at least two quarters so that initial conditions and the wage equation lag have no impact.[k]

The heavy line in Figure 4-2 traces out the long run Phillips curve tradeoff between unemployment and inflation implied by the CPA model under the assumptions we have listed. In contrast to the Phillips curves for the DLA and ILA models, it depicts the nonlinear, inverse relationship between unemployment and inflation characteristic of most Phillips curve studies. Additional increments in the rate of price inflation buy smaller and smaller decrements in the rate of unemployment as the economy approaches full employment and the labor market tightens.

Each annual unemployment-price inflation experience depicted by the light line time paths in Figure 4-2 can be thought of as lying on a short run Phillips curve, flatter in slope than the long run curve, which shifts position over time. That all of the simulated annual unemployment-inflation points lie below the long run Phillips curve, can be taken either as evidence that the U.S. has been more fortunate with its recent unemployment-inflation history than it has a right to expect over the long run, or as evidence that there are inconsistencies in the CPA model which surface in its long run implications.

----

simulations with it endogenous. The preliminary simulation results for the CPA model with RMP_t exogenous are presented in Table 4 of [5].

[k]Exactly what constant product market excess demand conditions means in the context of the CPA model is not clear. We have assumed it implies the ratio of UF_t to S_t is constant. Alternatives considered but rejected were that $(UF_t - UF_{t-1})/S_t$ takes on its mean value or is zero. The choice among these three alternatives had negligible impact on the CPA Phillips curve.

5

A Comparison of the Three Models

Before turning to an analysis of the freeze and Phase II, it is important that the similarities and differences among the DLA, ILA, and CPA mdoels presented in Chapters 2, 3, and 4, respectively, be evaluated. With knowledge of how the three models compare over our 1955:1 to 1971:2 historical period, we can undertake a more powerful assessment of controls using the models in concert than would be possible using each of them separately. Moreover, a comparison of the three models has intrinsic interest in itself, since they have all been estimated with a common data base for a common span of time.[a] This chapter undertakes that evaluation, framed around the distinguishing features of the models, the empirical properties of their individual equations, the simulations of them, and the long run Phillips curves implied by the mathematical solutions of them.

As applied in the last three chapters, the DLA, ILA, and CPA models have more in common than most models of the inflation process. First, they are based on a common body of data covering the same period from the first quarter of 1955 through the second quarter of 1971. Second, all of them use the same dependent variable in their price equations, namely the quarterly rate of change in the GNP implicit price deflator for the private, nonfarm economy. Third, two of the models use the same dependent variable in their wage equations, while the other model uses a similar one. The dependent wage variable in both the ILA and CPA models is the quarterly rate of change in the fixed weight gross index for production workers in the private, nonfarm economy, including fringe benefits and adjusted for interindustry employment shifts and manufacturing overtime; the dependent variable in the DLA wage equation is the rate of change in standard unit labor costs, which is the fixed weight gross wage index deflated by standard productivity. Finally, the models share many of the same explanatory variables, at least in general outline if not in exact specification.

Main Features of the Models

Notwithstanding their similarities, each model has certain features unique to itself. The DLA model:

1. incorporates Almon lags to capture the disequilibrium adjustments of wages and prices over time in response to movements in explanatory variables;

---

[a]As pointed out in Chapter 1, previous studies have reached widely disparate conclusions

2. uses standard unit labor costs as the dependent variable in the wage equation;

3. imposes an unusually long six-year lag on price expectations into the wage equation;

4. includes variables on changes in employee and employer taxes in the wage equation;

5. uses the short run divergence between output prices in general and consumer prices in particular to distinguish the labor demand and labor supply effects prices have on wages;

6. as originally formulated, uses a combination of three labor market variables to capture the impact of labor market conditions in the wage equation; and

7. uses standard unit labor costs as the only force driving prices in the long run, but allows productivity, product market demand pressures, and the ratio of total labor costs to standard ones to affect them in the short run.

Though patterned on the DLA model, the ILA departs from it in a number of respects. The ILA model:

1. imposes all lags as weighted averages of the current and past values of the variables involved;

2. employs a nonlinear price expectations effect in the wage equation by including both a weighted average of past consumer price changes to capture the "normal" impact and an inflation severity variable to capture the additional impact of rapid inflation;

3. takes employee tax changes into account, but ignores employer tax changes in the wage equation;

4. uses just the inverse of the unemployment rate to measure labor market tightness;

5. uses standard unit labor costs as the sole factor determining prices in the long run; and

6. allows wages, productivity, and product market demand conditions to have more complex impacts on prices in the short run than does the DLA model.

The CPA model differs substantially from the DLA and ILA models. It

1. minimizes the role of lags, allowing a simple Koyck lag in the wage equation, but no lag in the price equation;

2. uses productivity as an explanatory variable in both the wage and price equations;

---

concerning the inflation process based on different data covering different time periods. Thus, our replications with a common data base for a common time span provide a unique opportunity to focus solely on the specifications of the models. For the only other comparison of alternative models of which we are aware, see [19, pp. 385-404].

3. includes two unemployment variables in the wage equation to measure labor market conditions;

4. allows profits to affect wages;

5. makes no distinction between long and short run effects on prices;

6. allows raw materials prices to affect product prices in addition to unit labor costs, thereby allowing labor's share of income to vary; and

7. attempts to distinguish between demand and product market demand conditions which lower prices and raise them by using both capacity utilization and unfilled orders variables.

Empirical Estimates of the Models

The estimated wage and price equations for each of the three models appear in Table 5-1. The equations are grouped by models, with each equation marked by its original equation number.

The Wage Equations

Comparison of the standard errors and $\overline{R}^2$'s of the wage equations of the three models points up the superiority of both the original and modified DLA wage equations over the wage equations of the other two models. Both DLA wage Equations (2.3) and (2.4) have smaller standard errors and greater explanatory power corrected for degrees of freedom than either of the other wage equations. While the DLA wage equations are not strictly comparable with the other two wage equations because of differences in their dependent variables, explicitly taking this into account does not affect the comparison.[b]

The Durbin-Watson statistics for the ILA and CPA wage equations reveal no autocorrelation.[c] However, the Durbin-Watson statistic on the original DLA

---

[b]Theoretically, in the limit as $\Delta_t \to 0$, $(\dot{W}/Q^*)_t = \dot{W}_t - \dot{Q}^*_t = \dot{W}_t - K$, where K is a constant owing to the way $\dot{Q}^*_t$ is constructed. Consequently, reestimating the DLA wage equations with $\dot{W}_t$ used in place of $(\dot{W}/Q^*)_t$ should affect the standard error of the regressions slightly, but not the $\overline{R}^2$'s, except for rounding errors caused by the fact that t spans three months. An estimate of Equation (2.3) using $\dot{W}_t$ as the dependent variable conformed to this expectation, for it resulted in a standard error of 0.00189 and an $\overline{R}^2$ of 0.797. These statistics are identical to those of Equation (2.3). Estimation of Equation (3.3) with $(\dot{W}/Q^*)_t$ used as the dependent variable instead of $\dot{W}_t$ yielded an $\overline{R}^2$ of 0.676, identical to that of Equation (3.3) as originally estimated.

[c]The Durbin-Watson test is inappropriate for the CPA wage equation, because the lagged dependent variable appears as a regressor. As we noted in footnote g of Chapter 4, a corrected test for autocorrelation sustained the null hypothesis. See [1], [21, p. 307-314], and [31].

Table 5-1
Estimates of the DLA, ILA, and CPA Wage and Price Equations for the 1955:1 to 1971:2 Period
(with t-statistics in parentheses)

DLA Model

$$\left(\frac{\dot{W}}{Q^*}\right)_t = -0.0064 + 0.0129\,DU_t - 0.0029\,UD_t - 0.0559\,UH_t + 1.4410\,\dot{PCD}_{L,t}$$
$$(-2.71)\quad(1.98)\qquad(-0.05)\qquad(-0.88)\qquad(4.49)$$

$$+\,1.1405\,(P\dot{N}FD - \dot{PCD})_{L,t-1} + 0.0886\,T(\dot{E})_t + 1.1568\,T(\dot{F})'_t \qquad (2.3)$$
$$(3.08)\qquad\qquad\qquad(1.26)\qquad\qquad(4.90)$$

$$\overline{R}^2 = 0.797;\quad \text{D.W.} = 2.64;\quad \text{S.E.} = 0.00189$$

$$\left(\frac{\dot{W}}{Q^*}\right)_t = -0.0091 + 0.0003\left(\frac{1}{U}\right)_t + 1.6406\,\dot{PCD}_{L,t} + 0.4355\,(P\dot{N}FD - \dot{PCD})_{L,t-1}$$
$$(-4.61)\quad(3.28)\qquad\qquad(8.95)\qquad\qquad(1.38)$$

$$+\,0.0718\,T(\dot{E})_t + 1.1496\,T(\dot{F})'_t \qquad\qquad (2.4)$$
$$(0.97)\qquad\qquad(4.81)$$

$$\overline{R}^2 = 0.787;\quad \text{D.W.} = 2.42;\quad \text{S.E.} = 0.00194$$

$$P\dot{N}FD_t = 0.0009 + 0.9595\left(\frac{\dot{W}}{Q^*}\right)_{L,t} - 0.2933\left(\frac{\dot{Q}}{Q^*}\right)_{L,t} - 0.4246\left(\frac{\dot{W}}{CMH}\right)'_t$$
$$(1.23)\quad(6.54)\qquad\qquad(-2.06)\qquad\qquad(-2.26)$$

$$+\,0.0249\,\frac{U\dot{F}K}{UFK^*}_t \qquad\qquad (2.5)$$
$$(2.52)$$

$$\overline{R}^2 = 0.733;\quad \text{D.W.} = 2.40;\quad \text{S.E.} = 0.00208$$

ILA Model

$$\dot{W}_t = 0.0034 + 0.0003\left(\frac{1}{U}\right)_t + 0.1313\,\overline{\dot{PCD}}_t + 0.1725\,\dot{JP}_t + 0.0219\,\overline{T(\dot{E})}'_t$$
$$(2.24)\quad(3.84)\qquad(0.65)\qquad\qquad(3.77)\qquad(2.99)$$

$$-\,0.0019\,GP_t \qquad\qquad (3.3)$$
$$(-2.61)$$

$$\overline{R}^2 = 0.676;\quad \text{D.W.} = 2.22;\quad \text{S.E.} = 0.00241$$

$$PN\dot{F}D_t = 0.0006 + 0.8867\,(\dot{\bar{W}}_{t-1} - 0.0065) + 0.3749\,(\dot{W}_t - \dot{\bar{W}}_{t-1})$$
$$\phantom{PN\dot{F}D_t =} (1.04) \quad (10.00) \qquad\qquad\qquad (3.94)$$

$$-\,0.2284\,(\dot{\bar{Q}}_{t-1} - 0.0065) - 0.1268\,(\dot{Q}_t - \dot{\bar{Q}}_{t-1})$$
$$(-3.25) \qquad\qquad\qquad (-3.63)$$

$$-\,0.4199\,(\dot{\bar{W}}_t - \overline{CMH}_t) + 0.0547\,(UFK_t - UFK_{t-1})' \tag{3.4}$$
$$(-3.08) \qquad\qquad\qquad (1.76)$$

$$\bar{R}^2 = 0.733; \quad \text{D.W.} = 2.28; \quad \text{S.E.} = 0.00208$$

CPA Model

$$\dot{W}_t = 0.0021 + 0.0001\left(\frac{1}{U}\right)_t - 0.0021\,\dot{U}_t + 0.4992\,P\dot{C}D_t + 0.3202\,PN\dot{F}D_t$$
$$\phantom{\dot{W}_t =}(1.09) \quad (0.74) \qquad\quad (-0.34) \qquad (3.10) \qquad\quad (2.28)$$

$$+\,0.1070\,\dot{Q}_t + 0.0141\,\dot{C}_t + 0.2267\,\dot{W}_{t-1}$$
$$(1.98) \qquad (1.54) \qquad (2.21)$$

$$\bar{R}^2 = 0.663; \quad \text{D.W.} = 2.13; \quad \text{S.E.} = 0.00245 \tag{4.3}$$

$$PN\dot{F}D_t = -\,0.0011 + 0.6623\,\dot{W}_t - 0.1534\,\dot{Q}_t - 0.0024\,R\dot{M}P_t$$
$$\phantom{PN\dot{F}D_t =}(-1.16) \quad (9.27) \qquad (-3.28) \qquad (-0.22)$$

$$-\,0.0248\,C\dot{U}R_t + 0.0694\left(\frac{UF_t - UF_{t-1}}{S_t}\right)$$
$$(-1.32) \qquad\quad (2.08) \tag{4.4}$$

$$\bar{R}^2 = 0.639; \quad \text{D.W.} = 1.93; \quad \text{S.E.} = 0.00242$$

Source: Authors' estimates.

wage equation indicates serial correlation at the 5 percent confidence level, and that on the modified DLA equation is inconclusive. Since the presence of serial correlation produces both error measures biased downwards and inefficient estimates, the superiority of the DLA wage equations relative to the ILA and CPA ones is exaggerated by the OLS regression summary statistics presented in Table 5-1, but would be increased were generalized least squares used to eliminate the serial correlation problem for the DLA equations.[d]

[d]This problem may not be too severe, since the residuals are negatively correlated, not positively correlated. By leading to unduly large sampling variances of coefficient estimates when ordinary least squares techniques are employed, autocorrelated disturbances also produce inefficient predictions as well. Given the interaction between the wage and price equations in the simulations, this could explain why the DLA model ranks lower on the

The Price Equations

The price equations for the DLA and ILA models have identical $\bar{R}^2$'s and standard errors; the CPA price equation has less explanatory power and a larger standard error than these two counterparts by a wide margin. The Durbin-Watson statistic is insignificant at the 5 percent level for all three price equations, resulting in an acceptance of the null hypothesis regarding autocorrelation of their residuals.

Stability Tests

The outcome of stability tests on all the wage and price equations to determine if their regression coefficients are stable across subsets of the historical period have been briefly presented in Chapters 2, 3, and 4. Table 5-2 combines and compares results shown earlier in Tables 2-2, 3-1, and 4-1. On the one hand, the stability of the wage equations is inversely related to their explanatory power over the period as a whole. The DLA and ILA wage equations are unstable when the 1955:1 to 1965:4 and 1966:1 to 1971:2 subperiods are compared, but the CPA wage equation is stable over all subperiods tested. On the other hand, the stability of the price equations among subperiods corresponds directly to their explanatory power over the entire period. The DLA and ILA price equations are stable over all subperiods, while the CPA price equation is unstable when the subperiod ending in 1965 is compared with the one beginning in 1966.

We were unable to determine why the DLA and ILA wage equations are unstable; any number of factors could be responsible. One possibility is that the instability of the DLA and ILA wage equations stems from the structure of their price expectations variables.[1] The long lag on prices in the DLA wage equation and the inflation severity variable in the ILA wage equation both track the bulge in wages in the late sixties and early seventies, whereas the CPA wage equation with only a Koyck lag cannot track it. When the DLA wage equations and the ILA wage equation are estimated with shorter lags and without the inflation severity variable, respectively, their coefficients become stable over subsets of the historical period. However, these equations then underpredict wages beginning in the late sixties just as the CPA wage equation does. Thus, it could be that the long lag on prices in the DLA wage equation and the inflation severity variable in the ILA wage equation needed to track wages accurately over the entire 1955:1 to 1971:2 period introduce instability into the coefficients among subsets of that period.[e]

---

basis of the simulations than it does on the basis of the individual equations, as is pointed out in the following section. See [21, pp. 248-249, 265-266].

[e]The six-year lag on consumer prices in the DLA wage equation allows large wage and price

Table 5-2

F-Statistics for Tests of Equality on the DLA, ILA, and CPA Wage and Price
Equations across Subsets of the 1955:1 to 1971:2 Period
(with degrees of freedom in parentheses)

	Subperiods Tested		
	1955:1 to 1960:4 and 1961:1 to 1965:4	*1955:1 to 1965:4 and 1966:1 to 1971:2*	*1955:1 to 1960:4, 1961:1 to 1965:4 and 1966:1 to 1971:2*
Wage Equations:			
DLA Wage Equation (2.3)	0.79 (14,16)	1.99 (14,38)*	1.09 (28,24)
DLA Wage Equation (2.4)	1.36 (12,20)	2.24 (12,42)*	1.53 (24,30)
ILA Wage Equation (3.3)	1.21 (6,32)	2.65 (6,54)*	1.72 (12,48)
CPA Wage Equation (4.3)	1.18 (8,28)	1.63 (8,50)	1.28 (16,42)
Price Equations:			
DLA Price Equation (2.5)	0.98 (11,22)	1.19 (11,44)	1.04 (22,33)
ILA Price Equation (3.4)	0.90 (7,30)	1.35 (7,52)	1.07 (14,45)
CPA Price Equation (4.4)	0.92 (6,32)	2.75 (6,54)*	1.80 (12,48)

Source: Authors' estimates.

Note: GP_t and $\dot{J}P_t$ in the ILA wage equation are zero throughout the 1955:1 to 1960:4 and
the 1961:1 to 1965:4 subperiods, respectively. Each must be omitted from the ILA wage
equation covering the subperiod where it is constant in order to avoid a singular cross
product matrix which cannot be inverted. The omissions are ignored in the wage equation
tests of equality since they are made on account of the data, not as a priori restrictions on
the coefficients. For a discussion of the procedures used to compute these F-statistics, see
[8], [15], and [21, pp. 192-208].

*F-statistics significant at the 5 percent confidence level, but not at the 1 percent
confidence level.

In presenting the two versions of the DLA wage equation in Chapter 2, we
noted that its performance was relatively invariant with respect to the two
alternative specifications of the labor market variables and concluded that
multiple explanations appear to exist for the behavior of wages considered by
themselves during the 1955:1 to 1971:2 period. That the wage Equations (2.3)
and (2.4) exhibit the same stability patterns across subsets of the period
reinforces this conclusion.

Comparison of the Simulations and Mathematical Solutions

As we have argued in each chapter, the overall performance of each model

increases in the middle sixties to influence wage determinations in the early seventies.
Similarly, the inflation severity factor in the ILA wage equation allows abnormal changes in
prices to be counted twice.

cannot be satisfactorily evaluated without considering the interactions between the wage and price equations. Consequently, comparison of the simulation results and mathematical solutions previously presented in each chapter is necessary before final conclusions can be drawn, even though the DLA model using either wage Equation (2.3) or wage Equation (2.4) ranks first when looking at the individual wage and price equations.

Simulation Results

The estimated wage and price equations already described form the simulation basis for each model. In all three models we have closed wages and prices by introducing into the simulations Equation (2.6) linking PCD_t to an eight-quarter lag on $PNFD_t$. In addition, for the CPA model we have introduced Equation (4.5) linking RMP_t to a similar lag on $PNFD_t$. An identity has been used to transform the dependent variable of the DLA wage equation, the quarterly rate of change in standard unit labor costs, into the dependent variable of the ILA and CPA wage equations, the one-quarter rate of change in the fixed weight gross wage index, in order to render the wage changes simulated by all three models comparable.

Table 5-3 repeats the relevant error measures for the DLA, ILA, and CPA model simulations previously reported in Table 2-3, 3-2, and 4-2. Despite the fact that the DLA model ranks highest when examining the explanatory power and stability of the individual equations, Table 5-3 shows that this is not the case when examining the overall performances of the models in tracking wages and prices when interactions between their wage and price equations are allowed. Based on the simulation error measures reported in Table 5-3, the ILA model and the DLA model using wage Equation (2.4) must be judged superior to the DLA model using wage Equation (2.3) and the CPA model. This can be seen by looking at any of the error measures reported other than the mean errors.

The mean error indicates whether a model tracks above or below the actual values on average, but is a poor indicator of how well the model picks up fluctuations and turning points, because positive overprediction errors and negative underprediction errors cancel each other. As the mean errors in Table 5-3 show, the ILA and CPA models underpredict wages and prices on average, while the two versions of the DLA model overpredict on average. In comparing mean errors for both wages and prices, the CPA model ranks highest, the DLA model using wage Equation (2.3) lowest, and the ILA model and the DLA model using wage Equation (2.4) in between. On the average the CPA model simulation underpredicts the quarterly rates of change in both wages and prices by less than 0.001 percentage points. This accuracy contrasts sharply with the DLA model simulation using wage Equation (2.3), which overpredicts the rates of change in wages and prices by 1.2 and 0.59 percentage points per quarter, respectively.

Table 5-3
Error Measures for the 1955:1 to 1971:2 DLA, ILA, and CPA Models Simulations

	DLA Model Simulation Using Wage Equation (2.3)	DLA Model Simulation Using Wage Equation (2.4)	ILA Model Simulation	CPA Model Simulation
$\dot{W}_t$				
Mean Error	−0.0123581	−0.000416666	0.000258315	0.0000943516
Root Mean Square Error	0.0148448	0.00195670	0.00243844	0.00473728
Mean Absolute Error	0.0125076	0.00152937	0.00184676	0.00379961
Theil U Statistic	0.378992	0.076829	0.098736	0.190584
Regression of actual on simulated values	$\dot{W}_t = 0.0051 + 0.2814\,\hat{W}_t$ (5.62) (8.24) $\overline{R}^2 = 0.507$	$\dot{W}_t = -0.0012 + 1.0621\,\hat{W}_t$ (−1.37) (15.76) $\overline{R}^2 = 0.792$	$\dot{W}_t = -0.0012 + 1.1240\,\hat{W}_t$ (−1.01) (11.51) $\overline{R}^2\ 0.669$	$\dot{W}_t = 0.0090 + 0.2442\,\hat{W}_t$ (4.40) (1.45) $\overline{R}^2 = 0.017$
$PN\dot{F}D_t$				
Mean Error	−0.00592877	−0.000232183	0.0000772906	0.0000599409
Root Mean Square Error	0.00750554	0.00211660	0.00202668	0.00385734
Mean Absolute Error	0.00640130	0.00169993	0.00167657	0.00324394
Theil U Statistic	0.360682	0.148025	0.144987	0.278991
Regression of actual on simulated values	$PN\dot{F}D_t =$ $0.0008 + 0.4397\,\hat{PN\dot{F}D}_t$ (1.04) (8.25) $\overline{R}^2 = 0.508$	$PN\dot{F}D_t =$ $-0.0003 + 1.0061\,\hat{PN\dot{F}D}_t$ (−0.49) (12.95) $\overline{R}^2 = 0.720$	$PN\dot{F}D_t =$ $-0.0002 + 1.0533\,\hat{PN\dot{F}D}_t$ (−0.46) (13.71) $\overline{R}^2 = 0.742$	$PN\dot{F}D_t =$ $0.0026 + 0.5677\,\hat{PN\dot{F}D}_t$ (2.55) (3.64) $\overline{R}^2 = 0.159$

Source: Authors' estimates.

Note: The mean of $\dot{W}_t$ is 0.0119209; the mean of $PN\dot{F}D_t$ is 0.0059960. For a description of the error measure formulae, see the note to Table 2-3.

The mean absolute error and the root mean square error provide more meaningful measures of the tracking ability of a model than does the mean error. The mean absolute error avoids netting out overprediction and underprediction errors by using the absolute value of the difference between actual and predicted values; the root mean square error accomplishes the same thing by using the square of that difference. Although the two measures are approximately equivalent, the root mean square error is easier to work with mathematically. Moreover, it can be used to compare the accuracy of a simulation with the regressions on which the simulation is based. If the root mean square error for a simulated series is smaller than the standard error of the regression using that series as the dependent variable, then the residuals of the simulation will be more tightly clustered around zero than will the residuals of the estimated equations.[f]

Although the CPA model simulation has the smallest mean errors, only the DLA model simulation using wage Equation (2.3) has larger mean absolute and root mean square errors. The DLA model simulation using wage Equation (2.4) has the smallest mean absolute and root mean square errors for wages, while the ILA model has the smallest ones for prices. When the mean absolute errors for wages and prices are averaged to produce a composite mean absolute error for both wages and prices, the DLA simulation using wage Equation (2.4) comes out slightly better than the ILA model simulation, 0.160 percentage points to 0.175 percentage points per quarter. Similarly, when the root mean errors for wages and prices are averaged the DLA model simulation using wage Equation (2.4) comes out ahead, 0.204 percentage points to 0.223 percentage points per quarter. In contrast to these results, the DLA model simulation using wage Equation (2.3) and the CPA model simulation have composite mean absolute errors of 0.325 percentage points and 0.945 percentage points, respectively, per quarter.[g]

The Theil U statistic uses the root mean square error as its numerator, but adds a denominator which confines it to the (0,1) interval.[2] Given this similarity between the two error measures and the results for the root mean square errors, it is not surprising that the DLA model simulation using wage Equation (2.4) and the ILA model simulation have much smaller Theil U statistics than the CPA model simulation and the DLA model simulation using wage Equation (2.3).

---

[f]The root mean square error measures the dispersion of predicted values around the actual values for a series. The difference between the variance of a simulated series and its mean square error is the square of the mean error. If the mean of a simulated series is identical to the mean of the actual series, then the variance and the mean square error are identical; otherwise the mean square error must be larger. In a regression, where the mean of the predicted values of a series used as the dependent variable is constrained to equal the mean of its actual values, the mean square error of the series must equal its variance. See [23, p. 156].

[g]The composite mean absolute and root mean square errors for wages and prices were computed by adding the appropriate wage and price errors and dividing the sum that resulted by two. Such composite errors have no significance for statistical inference.

Where deterministic simulation of a model produces accurate predictions of a series, regressing the actual values of that series on the predicted values of it will yield an intercept term not significantly different from zero and a slope coefficient not significantly different from one.[3] Regressions of actual changes in wages and prices on their simulated values show that both the DLA model simulation using wage Equation (2.4) and the ILA model simulation did quite well. The $\bar{R}^2$'s are high, none of the intercepts are significantly different from zero, and none of the slope coefficients are significantly different from one. For the DLA model simulation using wage Equation (2.3) and the CPA model simulation the $\bar{R}^2$'s are considerably lower, the intercepts are significantly different from zero, and the slope coefficients are significantly different from one.

Long Run Phillips Curves

In Chapters 2, 3, and 4, we derived the long run Phillips curve for the DLA, ILA, and CPA models based on consistent sets of steady state assumptions. Differences among these Phillips curves provide insight as to why the simulations of the models differ in their ability to track inflation during the 1955:1 to 1971:2 period.

At one extreme, the DLA model using wage Equation (2.4) produces the positively sloped long run Phillips curve depicted in Figure 2-2. It is the same explosive price expectations impact in the DLA wage equation responsible for this positively sloped Phillips curve, which produces the cumulating overprediction of inflation in the DLA model simulation, using wage Equation (2.3) and the mean error overpredication in the DLA model simulation using wage Equation (2.4).

At the opposite extreme, the CPA model produces the traditional, negatively sloped long run Phillips curve shown in Figure 4-2. This shallow, downward sloping curve stems from the small roles played by unemployment and price expectations in the CPA wage equation and by wages in the CPA price equation. These are the same factors, particularly the small price expectations impact, that leave the model incapable of picking up the acceleration of inflation in the late 1960s.

In contrast to the Phillips curves for both the DLA and CPA models, the long run Phillips curve for the ILA model shown in Figure 3-3 is kinked. As long as the rate of price inflation does not exceed 2.5 percent per year, the ILA model Phillips curve is negatively sloped. When the rate of price inflation in the preceding two years exceeds 5 percent, or 2.5 percent per year, however, the inflation severity variable becomes positive reflecting an inflationary psychology, and the ILA Phillips curve becomes positively sloped. It is this same nonlinear price expectations impact responsible for the kinked Phillips curve, that allows the ILA model simulation to track the late sixties acceleration in the rate of inflation, without overpredicting wages and prices for the 1955:1 to 1971:2 period as a whole.

Choosing between the DLA model using wage Equation (2.4) and the ILA model on the basis of how well they simulate the 1955:1 to 1971:2 inflation experience is very difficult, for they perform about equally well. If anything, the DLA model would seem to have the edge on the basis of the smaller composite mean absolute and root mean errors considering wages and prices together. Considering the realism of the long run Phillips curves implied by the two models, however, we rate the ILA model slightly ahead. For, the kink in the ILA Phillips curve allows it to shift between "normal" and highly inflationary situations, while the DLA model using wage Equation (2.4) is locked into the latter situation.

The Wage and Price Impacts of
the Economic Stabilization
Program

In Chapter 5 we compared the DLA, ILA, and CPA models as presented in detail in Chapters 2, 3, and 4. The comparison considered both the performances of the individual equations of the models and the performances of the models on the whole. Our findings can be summarized as follows:

1. On the basis of the performances of the individual wage and price equations, the DLA model using either wage Equation (2.3) or wage Equation (2.4) ranks slightly ahead of the ILA model.

2. On the basis of the overall performances of the models in simulating the inflation experience of the 1955:1 to 1971:2 period, where dynamic interactions are allowed between wages and prices, there is no clear choice between the DLA model using modified wage Equation (2.4) and the ILA model. The DLA model using wage Equation (2.3) must be rejected.

3. On the basis of the long run Phillips curves implied by them, the ILA model emerges as preferred to the modified DLA model. The ILA model has a kinked Phillips curve capable of characterizing the long run tradeoff between unemployment and inflation in either "normal" or highly inflationary periods. In contrast, the Phillips curve implied by the modified DLA model always portrays the tradeoff only as if the latter situation existed.

4. The performance of the CPA model does not measure up to the performances of the DLA and ILA models, whether considering the structural equations or the dynamic simulations.

In this chapter we extend the analysis through 1972:4 in order to study the wage and price effects of controls. The extra six quarters starting with 1971:3 coincide closely with the 90-day freeze and the Phase II components of the Economic Stabilization Program: the 90-day wage-price freeze lasted from the second half of the third quarter to the first half of the fourth quarter in 1971, and Phase II lasted for the remainder of the fourth quarter in 1971 and all of 1972.[a]

Four procedures were followed in extending the models. First, we extended the simulations of our three models as estimated for the 1955:1 to 1971:2

---

[a]Controls were imposed on August 15, 1971, with the announcement of a 90-day freeze on all wages and prices. A more flexible Phase II controls program became effective on November 14, 1971. It continued in effect until superseded on January 11, 1973, by a self-enforced Phase III program intended to initiate decontrol.

period to cover the six additional quarters of the controls through 1972:4. The simulated wage and price changes for these six quarters were compared with the wage and price changes that actually occurred in order to detect shifts in the rates of wage and price change related to controls. For the DLA model we extended only the simulation relying on modified wage Equation (2.4), because that using wage Equation (2.3) did not perform satisfactorily in the precontrols period.[b]

Second, we introduced a dummy variable designed to represent the Economic Stabilization Program and reestimated the structural equations of the three models for the extended period including the six additional quarters of the freeze and Phase II. These reestimated equations, which we have labelled the controls equations in order to distinguish them from the historical equations previously presented for the 1955:1 to 1971:2 historical period, were used to measure the direct impacts of controls on wages and prices. Consistent with the extensions of our historical models simulations, we did not reestimate DLA wage Equation (2.3).

Third, we simulated the DLA, ILA, and CPA models for the 1971:3 to 1972:4 time span using the reestimated controls equations. These simulations, which we have labelled the controls models simulations in order to distinguish them from related simulations of the precontrols versions of the models, were utilized together with the extensions of the historical model simulations to measure the overall impacts which controls had on wages and prices during the freeze and Phase II.

Finally, we derived the long run Phillips curves implied by the reestimated controls versions of the wage and price equations of the three models. These Phillips curves were compared with those previously presented for the precontrols versions of the models in order to obtain insight into how controls shifted the steady state tradeoff between unemployment and inflation.

Extensions of the Historical Model Simulations

In previous chapters we have estimated the DLA, ILA, and CPA models over a period which ended prior to the inauguration of the Economic Stabilization Program. Two of these models, the modified DLA model using wage Equation

---

[b]The data series for DU_t, UD_t, and UH_t utilized in estimating wage Equation (2.3) over the 1955:1 to 1971:2 period were obtained from the individuals who originally constructed these series, as noted in Appendix B. Extending the DLA model simulation using wage Equation (2.3) would have necessitated extending these three data series. We calculated values for the three series over the added six quarters based on detailed instructions provided to us by the individuals originally responsible for the series, but were unable to reconcile our results with theirs. Given this problem in addition to the poor performance of the DLA model simulation using wage Equation (2.3), we elected not to extend this simulation when studying controls.

(2.4) and the ILA model, accurately simulate the acceleration of wages and prices in the late 1960s and early 1970s. If wages and prices were determined in the same manner after controls went into effect as they were prior to controls, then at least the two models which accurately predict wages and prices in the period up to 1971:2 could be expected to accurately predict the movement of wages and price during the period of controls. This implies that the error measures computed for simulations of these models over the precontrols and controls periods should be of approximately the same sign and magnitude. If the historical period relationships ceased to hold in the period of controls, however, then the error measures for the precontrols should differ from those for the controls period simulations.

Employing actual values in 1971:2 and earlier as the initial values of all variables in order to avoid introducing any simulation errors for the period prior to the establishment of controls, we simulated the historical models over the 1971:3 to 1972:4 period to test whether wage and price impacts assignable to the freeze and Phase II could be found. Table 6-1 presents the error measures for the 1971:3 to 1972:4 controls period simulations of the DLA model using wage Equation (2.4), the ILA model, and the CPA model. Comparison of these error measures with the smaller ones reported in Table 5-3 for the 1955:1 to 1971:2 simulations of the same models shows that the simulations track much more accurately in the precontrols period than in the controls period. This suggests, at least on the prima facie basis proposed in the previous paragraph, that the mechanisms generating wages and price were shifted by the 90-day freeze and Phase II.

The simulated wage and price changes predicted by the historical models for the six quarters 1971:3 through 1972:4 are characteristic of an economy without any controls program, while the actual wage and price changes occurred in an economy having such a program. Consequently, the mean errors reported for each model in Table 6-1 not only indicate relative to those reported for each model in Table 5-3 that controls affected wages and prices, but also provide in their own right one set of alternative measures of the size of the effects.[1]

Controls had a quite favorable impact on inflation according to the DLA model simulation, for its mean errors indicate a 1.27 percentage point reduction in the annual rate of wage growth and a 2.58 percentage point reduction in the annual rate of price increase. However, the ILA and CPA models simulations imply mixed effects less flattering to the controls program. The ILA model simulation mean errors indicate a 0.51 percentage point increase in the annual rate of wage growth and a 1.56 percentage point reduction in the annual rate of price increase, while the CPA model simulation indicates a 1.68 percentage point increase in the annual rate of wage growth and a 0.22 percentage point reduction in the annual rate of price increase. All three models imply that workers' real wage rates advanced as a result of wage and price controls, since they all indicate controls held down prices more than wages.

The mean errors reported in Table 6-1 estimate the wage and price impacts of controls inaccurately, because the difference between the wage and price changes predicted by the 1971:3 to 1972:4 simulations and the changes which actually took place cannot realistically be attributed solely to the influence of the Economic Stabilization Program. Table 5-3 shows that for the 1955:1 to 1971:2 historical period the DLA model simulation overpredicts on average, while the ILA and CPA models simulations underpredict on average. This suggests that they also predict with errors what would have happended during the 1971:3 to 1972:4 period in the absence of controls. Although Table 5-3 suggests the underprediction and overprediction errors are minor, a method of dealing with them is developed later in the chapter.[c]

Had we simulated the DLA, ILA, and CPA models over the 1971:3 to 1972:4 period simply by continuing our historical period simulations previously undertaken for the 1955:1 to 1971:2 period, simulation error cumulation problems would have arisen in addition to the underprediction and overpredic-

Table 6-1
Error Measures for the 1971:3 to 1972:4 DLA, ILA, and CPA Historical Models Simulations

	DLA Model Simulation Using Wage Equation (2.4)	ILA Model Simulation	CPA Model Simulation
$\dot{W}_t$			
Mean Error	−0.00317791	0.00128495	0.00420495
Root Mean Square Error	0.00412966	0.00387251	0.00522975
Mean Absolute Error	0.00319352	0.00326995	0.00420495
$P\dot{N}FD_t$			
Mean Error	−0.00645190	−0.00391148	−0.000542559
Root Mean Square Error	0.00705846	0.00469848	0.00256692
Mean Absolute Error	0.00645190	0.00391148	0.00194350

Source: Authors' estimates.

Note: The mean of $\dot{W}_t$ is 0.0156177; the mean of $P\dot{N}FD_t$ is 0.00428515. For a description of the error measures formulae, see the note to Table 2-3. We have omitted the Theil U statistics and the regressions of actual on simulated values owing to the shortness of the simulations period.

---

[c]A simple adjustment can be made by subtracting each mean error reported in Table 5-3 from the corresponding mean error reported in Table 6-1. Mean errors adjusted in this fashion are reported in Table 6-6. However, the validity of such an adjustment rests on the assumption that the extent of the overprediction or underprediction errors for the 1955:1 to 1971:2 and 1971:3 to 1972:4 simulations are the same. Comparison of the controls models simulations mean errors reported in Tables 6-5 and E-4 indicates such an assumption is unwarranted.

tion problems just mentioned. Tables E-1 and E-2 in Appendix E report the error measures which resulted from continuing our historical period simulations through the 1971:3 to 1972:4 controls period. Comparison of these error measures with those reported in Table 6-1 demonstrates how the compounding of the earlier period simulation errors introduces downward biases into the estimates of the salubrious impacts controls had on wage and price changes.[d]

Dummy Variable Estimates of the Direct Wage and Price Impacts

Another way to measure the wage and price impacts of the Economic Stabilization Program is to reestimate the wage and price equations of the DLA, ILA, and CPA models over the 1955:1 to 1972:4 extended period including controls with variables which serve as proxies for the 90-day freeze and Phase II introduced into the equations. We have done this by adding to all the wage and price equations the dummy variable ESP_t which takes on the value one for observations during controls and the value zero for all other observations. The approach is exactly analogous to that taken with GP_t in the ILA wage equation to measure the effectiveness of the wage-price guidelines of the middle sixties. ESP_t is not designed to explain the wage and price impacts of the freeze and Phase II, only to measure them.[2]

Dummy variables capture the influences which excluded factors have on the residuals of estimated equations. Although typically interpreted as proxies for particular factors, they sometimes actually represent forces other than those they are intended to represent. *Ex post* studies of the wage-price guideposts of the 1960s have produced contradictory evidence as to the magnitude of their impact, for instance, based on alternative dummy variable formulations.[3] It is entirely possible that future evaluations of the Economic Stabilization Program will prove similarly inconsistent. The intercept dummy ESP_t could be proven an inadequate proxy for measuring the controls program wage and price impacts, for example, or our association of it with the controls program could be shown to mask its true association with some other factor, or factors, which began to affect wages and prices roughly coincident with the establishment of controls.[e]

---

[d]Figures 2-1, 3-2, and 4-1 show that the DLA, ILA, and CPA models all track below the actual rates of wage and price change on average for the last year or two of the 1955:1 to 1971:2 simulations. Simulating the models over the 1971:3 to 1972:4 period by continuing the 1955:1 to 1971:2 simulations thus starts from a base of lower initial values than does starting from the actual values in 1971:2 and earlier. The lower base increases the algebraic value of the mean errors for the 1971:3 to 1972:4 simulations. Since the estimated impacts of the controls program vary inversely with the algebraic values of these mean errors, this has the effect of lowering the estimated impacts of the controls programs.

[e]Claims have been made that slope dummies are called for as well as intercept dummies in

Table 6-2
Estimates of the DLA, ILA, and CPA Controls Wage and Price Equations Containing ESP_t for the 1955:1 to 1972:4 Period
(with t-statistics in parentheses)

DLA Controls Model

$$\left(\frac{\dot{W}}{Q^*}\right)_t = -\,0.0093 + 0.0003\left(\frac{1}{U}\right)_t + 1.6733\,\dot{PCD}_{L,t} + 0.3065\,(\dot{PNFD}-\dot{PCD})_{L,t-1}$$
$$(-4.43)\quad(3.16)(8.52)(0.91)$$

$$+\,0.06729\,T(\dot{E})_t + 1.2489\,T(\dot{F})'_t - 0.0012\,ESP_t \tag{6.1}$$
$$(0.93)(4.92)(-0.80)$$

$$\overline{R}^2 = 0.754;\quad \text{D.W.} = 2.35;\quad \text{S.E.} = 0.00210$$

$$\dot{PNFD}_t = 0.0009 + 0.9515\left(\frac{\dot{W}}{Q^*}\right)_{L,t} - 0.2694\left(\frac{\dot{Q}}{Q^*}\right)_{L,t} - 0.4200\left(\frac{\dot{W}}{CMH}\right)_t$$
$$(1.27)\quad(6.67)(-1.83)(-2.29)$$

$$+\,0.0210\left(\frac{\dot{UFK}}{UFK^*}\right)_t - 0.0049\,ESP_t \tag{6.2}$$
$$(2.14)(-2.95)$$

$$\overline{R}^2 = .718;\quad \text{D.W.} = 2.51;\quad \text{S.E.} = .00211$$

ILA Controls Model

$$\dot{W}_t = 0.0034 + 0.0003\left(\frac{1}{U}\right)_t + 0.2381\,\overline{\dot{PCD}}_t + 0.1367\,\dot{JP} + 0.0206\,\overline{T(\dot{E})}_t$$
$$(2.13)\quad(3.44)(1.11)(2.91)(3.01)$$

$$-\,0.0020\,GP_t + 0.0027\,ESP_t \tag{6.3}$$
$$(-2.60)(2.32)$$

$$\overline{R}^2 = 0.643;\quad \text{D.W.} = 2.14;\quad \text{S.E.} = 0.00256$$

$$\dot{PNFD}_t = 0.0007 + 0.8734\,(\dot{W}_{t-1} - 0.0065) + 0.4554\,(\dot{W}_t - \overline{\dot{W}}_{t-1})$$
$$(1.19)\quad(9.93)(5.39)$$

$$-\,0.2330\,(\dot{Q}_{t-1} - 0.0065) - 0.1377\,(\dot{Q}_t - \overline{\dot{Q}}_{t-1}) - 0.4310\,(\overline{\dot{W}}_t - \overline{\dot{CMH}}_t)$$
$$(-3.33)(-4.04)(-3.19)$$

$$+\,0.0485\,(UFK_t - UFK_{t-1})' - 0.0039\,ESP_t \tag{6.4}$$
$$(1.51)(-3.38)$$

$$\overline{R}^2 = 0.726;\quad \text{D.W.} = 2.36;\quad \text{S.E.} = 0.00208$$

CPA Controls Model

$$\dot{W}_t = 0.0031 + 0.0000 \left(\frac{1}{U}\right)_t - 0.0079 \, \dot{U}_t + 0.4293 \, \dot{PCD}_t + 0.4810 \, \dot{PNFD}_t$$
$$(1.61) \quad (0.14) \qquad (-1.49) \qquad (2.69) \qquad (3.70)$$

$$+ 0.1670 \, \dot{Q}_t - 0.0016 \, \dot{C}_t + 0.1863 \, \dot{W}_{t-1} + 0.0025 \, ESP_t \qquad (6.5)$$
$$(3.79) \qquad (-0.60) \qquad (1.91) \qquad (1.80)$$

$$\overline{R}^2 = 0.656; \quad \text{D.W.} = 2.12; \quad \text{S.E.} = 0.00252$$

$$\dot{PNFD}_t = -0.0012 + 0.6687 \, \dot{W}_t - 0.1518 \, \dot{Q}_t - 0.0024 \, \dot{RMP}_t - 0.0253 \, \dot{CUR}_t$$
$$(-1.32) \quad (9.95) \qquad (-3.38) \qquad (-0.24) \qquad (-1.40)$$

$$+ 0.0701 \left(\frac{UF_t - UF_{t-1}}{S_t}\right) - 0.0032 \, ESP_t \qquad (6.6)$$
$$(2.19) \qquad\qquad\qquad (-2.93)$$

$$\overline{R}^2 = 0.651; \quad \text{D.W.} = 1.96; \quad \text{S.E.} = 0.00235$$

Source: Authors' estimates.

Table 6-2 presents the reestimated controls versions of the DLA, ILA, and CPA wage and price equation.[f] The coefficients on ESP_t in these equations provide alternative estimates of the direct impacts which the freeze and Phase II had in tandem on the rates of wage and price change. The coefficients measure only the direct impacts, rather than the total ones, because the wage and price equations standardize for price expectations and unit labor costs, respectively, and allow for no dynamic interactions between wages and prices. While the direct impacts on wages and prices implied by the coefficients on ESP_t could be attributed to the separate actions of the Pay Board and Price Commission, explaining how income policies affect the behavior of wages and prices, because income policies twist the Phillips curve in addition to shifting it. While it would be desirable to include slope dummies in the controls wage and price equations along with ESP_t, our ability to do this is constrained by the fact that only six observations in our extended 1955:1 to 1972:4 period correspond to the period when controls were in effect. Our simulations of the controls models should pick up via the interactions of wages and prices at least some of any Phillips curve twist. For discussions of the role of dummy variables in studying income policies, see [36] and [39, pp. 12-14].

[f]Individual distributed lag coefficients for Equations (6.1) and (6.2) are reported in Table E-3 of Appendix E.

respectively, we hesitate to assign them in such a fashion owing to the uncertainties noted in preceding paragraphs regarding the interpretations of dummy variables.

All three of the controls price equations in Table 6-2 have coefficients on ESP_t significantly negative at the 1 percent confidence level in one-tailed tests. Thus, they unanimously credit controls with having reduced the rate of price change given the rate of wage change. The estimates of this impact on an annual basis range from a 1.28 percentage point reduction for the CPA controls price equation to a 1.96 percentage point reduction for the DLA controls price equation, with the 1.56 percentage point reduction for the ILA controls price equation falling in the middle.

The coefficients on ESP_t in the controls wage equations of Table 6-2 offer conflicting testimony as to the direct impacts controls had on the rate of wage change. The significantly positive coefficients on ESP_t in the ILA and CPA controls wage equations imply that the Economic Stabilization Program raised the rate of wage change given the rate of price change, while the insignificantly negative coefficient on ESP_t in the DLA controls wage equation indicates that the freeze and Phase II had little effect on the rate of change in standard unit labor costs. The coefficients in the ILA and CPA controls wage equations indicate a 1.08 and 1.00 percentage point increase in the annual rate of wage change and are significant in one-tailed tests at the 1 and 5 percent confidence levels, respectively, but the insignificant coefficient in the DLA controls wage equations suggests a 0.48 percentage point reduction in the annual rate of standard unit labor cost change.[g]

Table 6-3 reports the results of stability tests performed on the controls equations over selected subsets of the 1955:1 to 1972:4 period involving the six quarters of controls. All of the equations are stable across the subperiods tested, notwithstanding the instability reported in Table 5-2 for some historical equations across certain subsets of the 1955:1 to 1971:2 precontrols period.

Simulations of the Controls Models Containing ESP_t

The ESP_t coefficients reported in Table 6-2 misstate the total effects which the Economic Stabilization Program had on wages and prices during the 90-day freeze and Phase II, because they ignore the wage and price feedback dynamics of the inflation process in two ways. One, they fail to take account of the fact that controls indirectly held down wages by holding down prices and thereby reducing inflationary price expectations. Two, they overlook the impact any wage effect would have on prices inasmuch as wages constitute the single most

---

[g]At first, the rapid productivity spurt that occurred during the early stages of the controls program and the different roles accorded to productivity in the dependent variables would

Table 6-3

F-Statistics from Tests of Equality on the DLA, ILA, and CPA Controls Wage and Price Equations Containing ESP_t across Subsets of the 1955:1 to 1972:4 Period

(with degrees of freedom in parentheses)

	Subperiods Tested		
	1955:1 to 1965:4 and 1966:1 to 1972:4	1955:1 to 1960:4, 1961:1 to 1965:4 and 1966:1 to 1972:4	1955:1 to 1971:2 and 1971:3 to 1972:4
Wage Equations:			
DLA Controls Wage Equation (6.1)	1.49 (13,46)	0.92 (26,33)	2.44 (6,53)
ILA Controls Wage Equation (6.3)	1.96 (7,58)	1.22 (14,51)	2.23 (6,59)
CPA Controls Wage Equation (6.5)	1.14 (9,54)	0.90 (18,45)	1.35 (6,57)
Price Equations:			
DLA Controls Price Equation (6.2)	0.83 (12,48)	0.75 (24,36)	1.05 (6,54)
ILA Controls Price Equation (6.4)	0.80 (8,56)	0.71 (16,48)	0.78 (6.58)
CPA Controls Price Equation (6.6)	2.06 (7,58)	1.37 (14,51)	0.15 (6,59)

Source: Authors' estimates.

Note: GP_t and JP_t in the ILA equation are zero throughout the 1955:1 to 1960:4 and the 1961:1 to 1965:4 subperiods, respectively, while ESP_t is zero in all equations throughout all subperiods ending in 1971:2 or earlier. Each must be omitted from the affected equations covering subperiods where it is constant in order to avoid a singular cross product matrix which cannot be inverted. The omissions are ignored in the tests of equality since they are made on account of the data, not as a priori restrictions on the coefficients. The tests of equality involving the 1971:3 to 1972:4 subperiod reflect the fact that the controls equations cannot be estimated for that subperiod owing to inadequate degrees of freedom. For a discussion of the procedures used to compute these F-statistics, see [8], [15], and [21, pp. 192-208].

---

seem to offer one possible explanation for the discrepancy between the impacts of ESP_t in the ILA and CPA controls wage equations versus in the DLA controls wage equation. However, we are at a loss in explaining how these two factors could explain the discrepancy. $(\dot{W}/Q^*)_t$ in the DLA controls wage equation uses Q^* defined on the basis of what happened only up to 1971:2, as can be seen from the definition of Q_t^* in Appendix A. This causes Q_t^* to be too small and $(\dot{W}/Q^*)_t$ to be too large for the period when productivity spurted soon after controls were introduced. $(\dot{W}/Q^*)_t$ being too large during controls would cause the coefficient on ESP_t to be too big in the DLA controls wage equation, whereas it is in fact much smaller than those in the ILA and CPA controls wage equations.

important cost element determining prices. Simulating the reestimated controls versions of the DLA, ILA, and CPA models provides a means of incorporating such interaction effects when measuring the total wage and price impacts controls had. In conjunction with the extensions of the historical models simulations presented earlier in the chapter, such simulations also afford a means of surmounting the underprediction and overprediction problems involved in interpreting those extensions of the historical models simulations.

We have simulated the controls models over the 1955:1 to 1972:4 period, and the 1955:1 to 1971:2 subset thereof, in order to check the performances of these simulations against those of the historical models simulations and then over the 1971:3 to 1972:4 period in order to measure the total wage and price impacts of controls. All of the controls models simulations are based on the reestimated controls wage and price equations of Table 6-2 as linked together in closed models with the same linking equations described in Chapters 2, 3, and 4.

Table 6-4 reports the relevant error measures for the 1955:1 to 1972:4 simulations of the controls models. The root mean square errors, mean absolute errors, and Theil U statistics for the CPA controls model are all inferior to those for the other two controls models. In addition, the root mean square errors for wages and prices in the CPA controls model are considerably larger than the standard errors of the CPA controls wage and price equations, whereas this is not the case for the DLA and ILA controls models. These findings, consistent with those of Chapter 5, indicate that less confidence can be placed in inferences about the Economic Stabilization Program impacts drawn from the CPA controls model simulations than from the DLA amd ILA controls models simulations.

Comparison of the Table 6-4 error measures with those presented in Table 5-3 shows that the controls models simulations perform about as well over the period for which the controls wage and price equations were estimated as the historical models simulations do over the period for which the precontrols wage and price equations were estimated.[h] The similarity of the mean errors reported in the two tables is especially important, owing to the underprediction and overprediction problem that arises in measuring the impact of the controls program. For practical purposes the underprediction and overprediction errors associated with the controls models and historical models simulations appear comparable enough and small enough to ignore, when using the differences between the corresponding mean errors for these two classes of simulations to

---

[h]Comparison of the Table E-4 error measures with those presented in Table 5-3 shows that the historical models simulations perform slightly better than the controls models simulations for the 1955:1 to 1971:2 precontrols period. This is to be expected, since the historical wage and price equations were estimated for that period, while the controls wage and price equations were estimated for the 1955:1 to 1972:4 extended period. Given that the superiority of the historical models simulations for the precontrols period is marginal, we view it as unimportant in estimating the impact of the Economic Stabilization Program.

Table 6-4
Error Measures for the 1955:1 to 1972:4 DLA, ILA, and CPA Controls Models Simulations

	DLA Controls Model Simulation	ILA Controls Model Simulation	CPA Controls Model Simulation
$\dot{w}_t$			
Mean Error	−0.000328491	0.000338978	0.000424635
Root Mean Square Error	0.00217439	0.00267846	0.00534292
Mean Absolute Error	0.00166993	0.00198689	0.00440281
Theil U Statistic	0.0836603	0.106156	0.212535
Regression of actual on simulated values	$\dot{w}_t = -0.000920 + 1.04\,\hat{w}_t$ (−0.97)　(14.38) $\overline{R}^2 = 0.743$	$\dot{w}_t = -0.000609 + 1.09\,\hat{w}_t$ (−0.55)　(10.68) $\overline{R}^2 = 0.610$	$\dot{w}_t = 0.0129 - 0.0530\,\hat{w}_t$ (6.30)　(−0.32) $\overline{R}^2 = 0.012$
$P\dot{N}FD_t$			
Mean Error	−0.000205624	0.000126152	0.000275407
Root Mean Square Error	0.00208055	0.00211287	0.00424840
Mean Absolute Error	0.00165537	0.00175630	0.00360752
Theil U Statistic	0.148581	0.158588	0.315527
Regression of actual on simulated values	$P\dot{N}FD_t =$ $-0.000144 + 0.989\,P\hat{N}FD_t$ (−0.28)　(13.57) $\overline{R}^2 = 0.721$	$P\dot{N}FD_t =$ $0.000892 + 1.006\,P\hat{N}FD_t$ (0.18)　(13.23) $\overline{R}^2 = 0.710$	$P\dot{N}FD_t =$ $0.00374 + 0.378\,P\hat{N}FD_t$ (4.09)　(2.65) $\overline{R}^2 = 0.078$

Source: Authors' estimates.
Note: The mean of $\dot{w}_t$ is 0.0122289; the mean of $P\dot{N}FD_t$ is 0.00585343. For a description of the error measures formulae, see the note to Table 2-3.

measure the overall wage and price impacts of the freeze and Phase II. The corresponding mean errors reported in Tables 6-4 and 5-3 all have the same signs and quite similar magnitudes, although this is true to a lesser degree for the CPA models simulations than for the others. Moreover, this same impression is sustained for just the 1955:1 to 1971:2 period, as can be seen by comparing the mean errors reported in Table E-4 of Appendix E for the 1955:1 to 1971:2 subset of the controls models simulations with those reported in Table 5-3.

Table 6-5 reports the error measures for simulations of the controls models over the 1971:3 to 1972:4 period using actual values in 1971:2 and earlier as the initial values of all variables. The differences between the mean errors reported in Table 6-1 for the 1971:3 to 1972:4 simulations of the historical models and the corresponding mean error reported in Table 6-5, both based on the identical initial values, form a set of alternative estimates of the wage and price impacts of controls, approximately free of underprediction and overprediction problems.[i] Once again the DLA model presents the most favorable picture of controls, indicating a 1.49 percentage point reduction in the annual rate of wage growth and a 2.60 percentage point reduction in the annual rate of price increase. Both the ILA and CPA models indicate that controls raised the annual rate of wage growth by 0.10 percentage points, with the ILA model implying a 1.64 percentage point reduction and the CPA model implying a 1.20 percentage point reduction in the annual rate of price increase.[j]

---

[i]As has already been pointed out and made use of, the extensions of the historical models simulations trace out the hypothetical wage and price behavior for the case without controls. Since the controls models simulations trace out the wage and price behavior for the case with controls, and the extent of underprediction and overprediction errors with the two sets of simulations is approximately the same, the differences between the historical models and controls models simulations correspond to the wage and price impacts of controls. Using the Table 2-3 definition of the mean error, $1/T \sum_{t=1}^{t} (A_t - P_t)$, it is easy to demonstrate that the difference between the mean errors of two separate simulations of any series over the identical period equals the negative of the mean difference between the two sets of predictions:

$$\left\{ \frac{1}{T} \sum_{t=1}^{T} (A_t - P_t) \right\} - \left\{ \frac{1}{T} \sum_{t=1}^{T} (A_t - P_t^*) \right\} = \frac{1}{T} \sum_{t=1}^{T} (P_t^* - P_t)$$

Table E-6 in Appendix E reports the 1971:3 to 1972:4 predictions of wage and price change obtained with the historical models and controls models simulations, since these predictions are of interest in themselves.

[j]We could have derived an alternative set of estimates of the total wage and price impacts of controls by simulating the controls models over the 1971:3 to 1972:4 period with $ESP_t = 0$ instead of extending the historical models simulations. Such an approach would have eliminated the underprediction and overprediction problem entirely. However, we felt the historical models presented the wage and price mechanisms operating in the precontrols period slightly better. Using the historical models simulations allowed the coefficients other than those on ESP_t to differ somewhat in the cases with controls and without them. This permitted greater twisting of the Phillips curve such as mentioned in footnote e earlier in

Table 6-5

Error Measures for the 1971:3 to 1972:4 DLA, ILA, and CPA Controls Models Simulations

	DLA Controls Model Simulation	ILA Controls Model Simulation	CPA Controls Model Simulation
$\dot{W}_t$			
Mean Error	0.000558358	0.00102237	0.00344372
Root Mean Square Error	0.00316800	0.00405318	0.00529073
Mean Absolute Error	0.00258318	0.00370595	0.00405347
$\dot{PNFD}_t$			
Mean Error	0.0000544096	0.000200164	0.00296971
Root Mean Square Error	0.00244103	0.00258763	0.00371762
Mean Absolute Error	0.00428515	0.00191021	0.00316395

Source: Authors' estimates.

Note: The mean of $\dot{W}_t$ is 0.0156177; the mean of $\dot{PNFD}_t$ is 0.00428515. For a description of the error measures formulae, see the note to Table 2-3. We have omitted the Theil U statistics and the regressions of actual on simulated values owing to the shortness of the simulations period.

Controls Induced Shifts in the Long Run Phillips Curves

So far in this chapter we have presented estimates of the wage and price impacts which controls had during the six quarters of the 90-day freeze and Phase II as obtained with three alternative approaches. By deriving for the DLA, ILA, and CPA controls models the long run Phillips curves consistent with the Economic Stabilization Program and comparing them with Phillips curves applicable in the absence on controls, estimates can also be obtained of the steady state effects the freeze and Phase II would have had once conditions prior to the freeze had ceased to affect the rates of change in wages and prices.[k]

Using the same steady state assumptions as in Chapters 2, 3, and 4, we have simultaneously solved the reestimated wage and price equations containing ESP_t for each of the three controls models in order to derive the long run Phillips curves consistent with controls. Figures 6-1, 6-2, and 6-3 depict for the DLA,

---

this chapter. Ideally, we could have compared the extended historical model simulations with simulations based on wage and price equations estimated solely for the period of controls had there been sufficient observations with which to estimate the latter equations.

[k]In speaking of the long run wage and price impacts of the Economic Stabilization Program it is important to keep in mind that we are talking in this chapter about hypothetical steady state impacts, not the impacts which will survive the freeze and Phase II for a long time. Such long lasting impacts are covered in the next chapter.

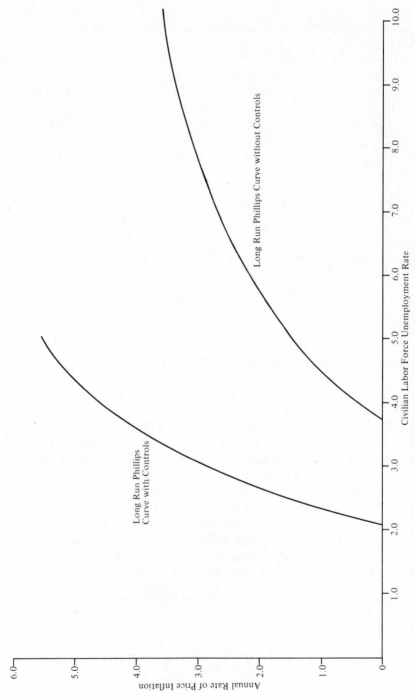

Figure 6-1. Long Run Phillips Curves for the DLA Model with and without Controls.

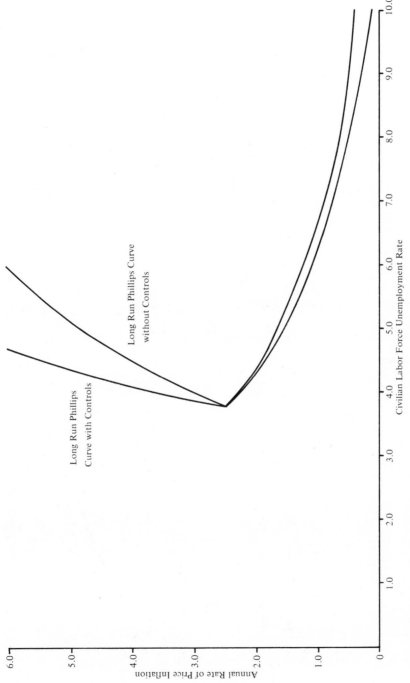

Figure 6-2. Long Run Phillips Curves for the ILA Model with and without Controls.

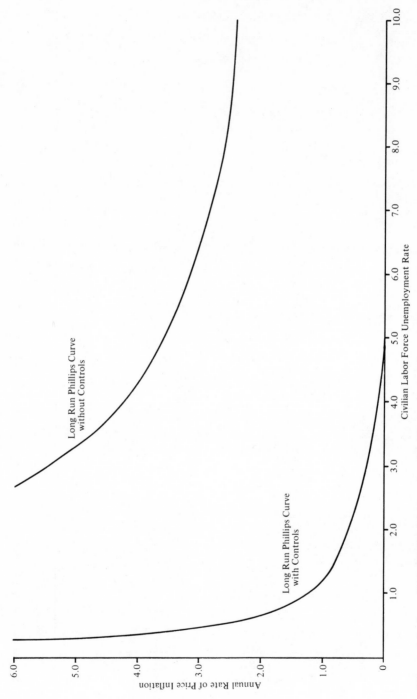

Figure 6-3. Long Run Phillips Curves for the CPA Model with and without Controls.

ILA, and CPA models, respectively, both these controls models Phillips curves and the 1955:1 to 1971:2 period historical models ones previously shown in Figures 2-2, 3-3, and 4-2. In each figure the Phillips curve representing the steady state tradeoff between unemployment and inflation in the absence of controls lies to the right of the Phillips curve representing the tradeoff consistent with the 90-day freeze and Phase II.[1] This indicates that the wage and price controls not only slowed inflation, but also reversed at least temporarily the adverse rightward drift of the Phillips curve which has characterized the U.S. economy in recent years.[4] For all three models the Phillips curves without controls lie somewhat farther to the right of the Phillips curves with controls at high rates of inflation than at low rates of inflation. This is consistent with the claim advanced elsewhere that incomes policies twist the Phillips curve, though hardly convincing, independent evidence of it given the small degree of twist detected.[5]

The long run Phillips curves implied by the controls models in the presence and absence of controls differ only because of the different values assigned to ESP_t in the two situations. Consequently, the change brought about in the steady state rate of price inflation by the introduction of the freeze and Phase II according to each controls model can be determined by taking the partial derivative of its Phillips curve equation with respect to ESP_t, where that equation is written with the rate of price change as the dependent variable. After simultaneously solving the controls wage and price equations of each model for the long run tradeoff between unemployment and the rate of wage growth instead of for the tradeoff between unemployment and the rate of price change as we have done up to here, the same procedure can be utilized to determine for each controls model the steady state change produced in the rate of wage growth.

For the DLA controls model and the ILA controls model in times of rapid inflation, the steady state changes in the rates of wage and price increase associated with the introduction of the Economic Stabilization Program are misleading, because, as originally discussed for the historical versions of the two models in Chapters 2 and 3, their Phillips curves are unstable. The DLA controls model implies a 63.48 percentage point rise in the annual rate of steady state wage growth and a 4.12 percentage point rise in the annual rate of steady state price increase, but neither steady state impact can be reached. The initial effect of introducing controls in the DLA controls model is to drive the rates of change in wages and prices down, as can be seen from the negative coefficients on ESP_t in Equations (6.1) and (6.2) of Table 6-2. This sets in motion a cumulating

---

[1]Analogously to the case of our controls models simulations, we could have obtained alternative estimates of the Phillips curves shifts by solving the controls models for them with $ESP_t = 0$ instead of using the historical models Phillips curves. Although not shown, the controls models Phillips curves with $ESP_t = 0$ are extremely similar to the historical models ones. We chose to report only these latter curves for simplicity and the reasons already given in footnote j of this chapter.

deflation owing to the destabilizing role of price expectations in wage Equation (6.1), reflected in the coefficient on $PCD_{L,t}$ exceeding one, which forces the changes in the rates of wage and price increase further and further from their steady state values over time.

The ILA controls model implies a 9.80 percentage point rise in the steady state annual rate of wage growth and a 1.72 percentage point rise in the steady state annual rate of price increase whenever prices have risen more than 5 percent in the preceding eight quarters. However, these impacts cannot be reached either. The initial effect of introducing controls is to drive the rate of change in wages up and the rate of change in prices down, as can be seen from the coefficients on ESP_t in Equations (6.3) and (6.4) of Table 6-2. When more than 5 percent inflation has occurred in the preceding eight quarters, this sets in motion a cumulating deflation owing to the destabilizing joint impact of $\overline{\dot{PCD}}_t$ and $\dot{JP}_t$ in wage Equation (6.3), driving the change in the rate of price increase and eventually that in the rate of wage growth down and further away from their steady state values over time.

For the ILA controls model in "normal" times, where prices have risen 5 percent or less in the previous two years, and the CPA controls model the steady state changes in the rates of wage and price increase are attainable. The ILA controls model in "normal" times implies a 0.92 percentage point rise in the annual rate of steady state wage growth and a 0.36 percentage point reduction in the annual rate of steady state price increase. The CPA controls model implies a 0.08 percentage point rise in the annual rate of steady state wage growth and a 1.72 percentage point reduction in the annual rate of steady state price increase.

Summary and Evaluation of Results

Table 6-6 summarizes our various estimates of the wage and price impacts which the Economic Stabilization Program had during the 90-day freeze and Phase II. In itself each of these estimates is subject to criticism. Nevertheless, with the exception of the steady state impacts which have little significance in some cases, as noted, these alternative estimates paint a consistent picture of the impacts controls had.

All of our approaches to measuring the impact of controls show that the rate of price inflation was reduced by controls. Taking into account the limited reliability of the CPA model results, the freeze and Phase II appear to have slowed the annual rate of price increase by more than one percentage point and perhaps more than two percentage points. Notwithstanding the limitations of the procedure used to adjust the mean errors, the very small differences between the mean errors for the extensions of the historical models simulations and the adjusted mean errors for them suggest how insignficant the underprediction and overprediction problem is in measuring the magnitude of the reduction in the rate of price inflation.

Table 6-6
Alternative Estimates in Percentage Points of the Impacts the Economic Stabilization Program Had on the Annual Rates of Change in Wages and Prices during the Freeze and Phase II

		DLA Models	ILA Models	CPA Models
	$\dot{W}_t$			
(1)	Mean errors for the 1971:3 to 1972:4 historical models simulations	− 1.27	+0.51	+1.68
(2)	Adjusted mean errors for the 1971:3 to 1972:4 historical models simulations	− 1.11	+0.41	+1.64
(3)	Controls wage equations coefficients on ESP_t	− 0.48	+1.08	+1.00
(4)	Differences between the mean errors for the 1971:3 to 1972:4 controls and historical models simulations	− 1.49	+0.10	+0.10
(5)	Partial derivatives of the controls models long run Phillips curves equations with respect to ESP_t	+63.48	+9.80 (inflationary periods) +0.92 ("normal" periods)	+0.08
	$PN\dot{F}D_t$			
(1)	Mean errors for the 1971:3 to 1972:4 historical models simulations	− 2.58	−1.56	−0.22
(2)	Adjusted mean errors for the 1971:3 to 1972:4 historical models simulations	− 2.49	−1.59	−0.24
(3)	Controls price equations coefficients on ESP_t	− 1.96	−1.56	−1.28
(4)	Differences between the mean errors for the 1971:3 to 1972:4 controls and historical models simulations	− 2.60	−1.64	−1.20
(5)	Partial derivatives of the controls models long run Phillips curves equations with respect to ESP_t	+ 4.12	+1.72 (inflationary periods) −0.36 ("normal" periods)	−1.72

Source: Authors' estimates.

Note: The adjusted mean errors for the 1971:3 to 1972:4 historical models simulations were obtained by subtracting from the mean errors for the 1971:3 to 1972:4 historical models simulations the mean errors for the corresponding 1955:1 to 1971:2 historical models simulations in order to take into account the underprediction and overprediction problem. See footnote c earlier in this chapter.

The different ways of measuring the impacts of controls yield estimates of the effect on the rate of wage change which are consistent in sign for each of the DLA, ILA, and CPA models considered by themselves, but are inconsistent for the DLA model as compared with the ILA and CPA model. The DLA model indicates the rate of change in standard unit labor costs was reduced by controls, while the ILA and CPA models indicate the rate of change in wages was increased. Again, the differences between the mean errors for the extensions of the historical models simulations and the adjusted mean errors for them suggest the relative unimportance of the underprediction and overprediction problem, even though the differences are larger in the case of wages than in the case of prices.

All of the controls models simulations indicate total wage impacts considerably smaller than the direct impacts indicated by the coefficient on ESP_t in the corresponding controls wage equations, reflecting the indirect contribution the reduction in the rate of price increase played in slowing down wages.[m] While no clear conclusion can be reached about either the sign or size of the impact controls had on the rate of wage change owing to the conflicts between the effects implied by the DLA model versus those implied by the ILA and CPA models, all three models indicate that the freeze and Phase II restrained the rate of wage increase less than the rate of price increase irrespective of the measurement approach.

---

[m]Reflecting the mixed effects controls had on wages, the controls modes simulations indicate price impacts both greater than and less than the direct impacts indicated by the coefficient on ESP_t in the corresponding controls price equations.

7 Implications of the Analysis

Forecasts for Phase III and Beyond

Up to this point our evaluation of the Economic Stabilization Program has centered on the impact controls had during the 90-day wage-price freeze and the successor to the freeze for 14 months, Phase II. The analysis has provided little insight into the longer lasting impacts of the freeze and Phase II. Thus, Chapter 6 showed that controls affected the quarterly rates of change in wages and prices for the private, nonfarm economy for the period from 1971:3 through 1972:4, but says nothing about how the freeze and Phase II influenced what happened in Phase III or later.

Events subsequent to January of 1973 raise serious questions as to whether controls slowed inflation from August of 1971 up until 1973 by eliminating inflationary pressures or merely suppressing them. The January exit of Phase II, together with the dusappearance of the Price Commission and the Pay Board, marked the entrance of Phase III and a more relaxed controls machinery intended to initiate decontrol of the economy. Following this change in policy and program, inflation accelerated rapidly—most obviously in food prices, but also throughout the rest of the private, nonfarm sector—until a new 60-day freeze on prices was imposed in June.[a] How much of this inflation reacceleration was the legacy of Phase II and how much the fruit of Phase III has been a subject of serious debate.[1]

Relaxing controls need not necessarily lead to an explosion of wages and prices. Under circumstances where the decontrol process is effective in fostering an atmosphere of voluntary restraint on the part of both business and labor to replace the mandatory restraint of controls, the decontrol period could experience the same movements in wages and prices as the controls period in the absence of suppressed inflationary pressures. Alternatively, where voluntary restraint is not achieved or suppressed inflationary pressures are present, decontrol is likely to be associated with an acceleration of inflation. When decontrol leads to the latter case, as it did in Phase III, the problem becomes one of discovering whether the spurt in inflation resulted from a " bubble" of suppressed inflation left behind by controls or from failures of the decontrol process itself.

---

[a]During Phase II the Consumer Price Index rose at an annual rate of 3.4 percent; during Phase III it rose at an annual rate of 8.1 percent. Excluding food, the rates of change were 2.8 percent and 4.0 percent. All figures are nonseasonally adjusted. See [3].

Unfortunately, whether the Phase III spurt in inflation should be attributed to the long run limitations of Phase II or to the failures of Phase III cannot be ascertained from analyses of the type presented in Chapter 6. Owing to the inability of our three inflation models to distinguish between the elimination of inflationary pressures and the suppression of these pressures, analyses of those models can provide no guidance as to what caused events in the postanalysis period.[b] In other words, Chapter 6 cannot tell us whether Phase II temporarily slowed inflation in the short run by distorting wages and prices without having had any substantial lasting influence.

In an effort to obtain a better picture of the long run impacts which the 90-day freeze and Phase II had on wages and prices, we have forecasted the quarterly rates of change in wages and prices from the first quarter of 1973 through the last quarter of 1974 with the controls versions of our three models under three different assumptions concerning the effectiveness of controls during that period. While any number of assumptions about the effectiveness of controls in 1973 and 1974 could have been utilized, we tested the three options: ESP_t = 1.0, a full impact; ESP_t = 0.5, a half impact; ESP_t = 0, a zero impact. The full impact option implies that no loss in the efficiency of controls occurred in moving from Phase II to later programs. The half impact option implies that the later programs were one half as effective as the 90-day freeze and Phase II. The zero option implies that controls became completely ineffective, equivalent to having no controls, starting with Phase III.

1973 and 1974 values for most of the exogenous variables which enter into the three inflation models were obtained directly from forecasts generated by the Data Resources, Inc. macroeconometric model of the U.S. economy. Values for two variables were so obtained indirectly.[c] In order to reflect the sensitivity of wages and prices to the unemployment rate, however, four alternative sets of forecasts were made for that rate. The values of the exogenous variables taken directly and indirectly from the Data Resources, Inc. model and our four

---

[b]The dummy variable ESP_t provides a measure of how the rates of change in wages and prices during the freeze and Phase II differed from what they would have been in the absence of the Economic Stabilization Program, but is not capable of explaining what caused the difference. See our discussion of ESP_t in Chapter 6 and the references cited there.

[c]We were unable to obtain forecasts of two exogenous variables used in the CPA model, S_t and UF_t. For these two variables we established a relationship to other, related variables for the period 1955:1 to 1972:4 and then used forecasts of these other variables to predict values of S_t and UF_t beginning in 1973:1. S_t, sales in manufacturing and trade, was regressed on GNP_t, gross national product,

$$S_t = 38.14 + 0.2881\ GNP_t.$$
$$(23.94)\quad (129.72)$$

$$\overline{R}^2 = 0.966;\ \text{D.W.} = 0.32;\ \text{S.E.} = 4.326$$

alternative sets of values for the unemployment rate are presented in Appendix F. In undertaking the forecast simulations, the actual values of the endogenous variables for the fourth quarter of 1972, and earlier where appropriate, were used as the initial values of these variables.

Thus, twelve different sets of forecasts of wage and price changes were prepared for the controls versions of each of our three models by matching the four sets of unemployment rate forecasts with the three assumptions on the effectiveness of controls.[d] Tables 7-1 through 7-4 report these forecasts. By choosing what he considers the most reasonable combination of forecasts and assumptions and seeing whether that choice leads to underpredicting or overpredicting the rates of change in wages and prices for 1973 and 1974, the reader can form his own judgments about the extent to which a "bubble" of suppressed inflationary pressure left behind by Phase II versus the ineffectiveness of subsequent phases caused the rate of inflation to accelerate in Phase III.

In assessing the long run impacts of the 90-day freeze and Phase II with the forecast of his choice, the reader should bear in mind four caveats. First, these *ex ante* forecasts are based on forecasted values of the exogenous variables; their accuracy depends on that of the exogenous variables forecasts. Second, our three options for the effectiveness of Phase III, the 60-day price freeze, Phase IV, and whatever else may follow make no allowance for differences among these post-Phase II programs. Significant differences cannot be simply averaged out, because of the dynamics involved in the inflation process. Third, and closely associated with the preceding point, the validity of the assumptions drawn with respect to Phase II will depend on selecting the right option with respect to the short run effectiveness of the controls programs subsequent to Phase II. Fourth, random noise in the inflation process and simulation errors, including simulation biases, should be kept in mind when drawing conclusions.

Ex post analyses should offer better opportunities to assess both the long run impacts of the 90-day freeze and Phase II and short and long run impacts of subsequent chapters of the Economic Stabilization Program.

UF_t, unfilled orders in manufacturing in current dollars, was regressed on RUF_t, real unfilled orders in manufacturing in 1958 dollars,

$$UF_t = -8.543 + 1.190 \, RUF_t.$$
$$(-2.58) \quad (22.27)$$

$$\overline{R}^2 = 0.875; \quad \text{D.W.} = 0.02; \quad \text{S.E.} = 4.962.$$

[d]These 12 forecasts implicitly assume that the exogenous variables other than the unemployment rate and the controls program dummy always take on the same values. This is unrealistic. For example, we would expect output per manhour and personal tax payments to change as the impact of the controls program changed. Accurately determining how these other variables would change is not an easy task, however. Therefore, we have assumed the exogenous variables to be constant under all circumstances in the interest of simplicity. For another approach based on alternative simplifying assumptions, see [27].

Table 7-1

Forecasts of $\dot{W}_t$ and $P\dot{N}FD_t$ at Quarterly Percentage Rates for High Unemployment Assumption

$ESP_t = 0$	DLA Controls Model		ILA Controls Model		CPA Controls Model	
	$\dot{W}_t$	$P\dot{N}FD_t$	$\dot{W}_t$	$P\dot{N}FD_t$	$\dot{W}_t$	$P\dot{N}FD_t$
73:1	2.33	1.06	0.88	0.61	−0.17	−1.11
73:2	1.37	0.94	1.32	0.73	0.85	0.53
73:3	1.56	0.89	1.26	0.74	1.47	0.90
73:4	1.60	0.92	1.09	0.69	1.72	1.11
74:1	1.90	1.09	1.12	0.65	1.66	1.00
74:2	1.73	1.01	1.13	0.61	1.75	1.07.
74:3	1.79	0.96	1.13	0.58	1.83	1.09
74:4	1.84	0.94	1.12	0.56	2.01	1.22
$ESP_t = 0.5$	$\dot{W}_t$	$P\dot{N}FD_t$	$\dot{W}_t$	$P\dot{N}FD_t$	$\dot{W}_t$	$P\dot{N}FD_t$
73:1	2.25	0.79	1.00	0.45	−0.19	−1.29
73:2	1.25	0.66	1.43	0.57	0.79	0.33
73:3	1.35	0.60	1.36	0.59	1.42	0.71
73:4	1.41	0.61	1.19	0.54	1.67	0.92
74:1	1.68	0.76	1.22	0.50	1.60	0.80
74:2	1.47	0.67	1.23	0.46	1.69	0.86
74:3	1.49	0.59	1.23	0.43	1.76	0.89
74:4	1.51	0.56	1.23	0.41	1.96	1.02
$ESP_t = 1.0$	$\dot{W}_t$	$P\dot{N}FD_t$	$\dot{W}_t$	$P\dot{N}FD_t$	$\dot{W}_t$	$P\dot{N}FD_t$
73:1	2.16	0.53	1.12	0.29	−0.22	−1.46
73:2	1.14	0.38	1.54	0.41	0.74	0.14
73:3	1.20	0.30	1.47	0.43	1.36	0.52
73:4	1.22	0.31	1.29	0.39	1.62	0.72
74:1	1.45	0.44	1.32	0.36	1.55	0.61
74:2	1.21	0.32	1.34	0.31	1.62	0.66
74:3	1.19	0.24	1.33	0.28	1.69	0.68
74:4	1.18	0.18	1.33	0.26	1.91	0.83

Source: Authors' estimates.

Conclusions

Our analyses of the DLA, ILA, and CPA models with a common body of data covering the same period reveals that how such models are formulated does affect how successfully they depict the inflation process. Most significantly, the specification of the lags involved and the role price expectations play emerge as important considerations, with the optimal specification of these influences and labor market influences seemingly a joint function of the specific context.

On the basis of our examination of the Economic Stablization Program with

Table 7-2

Forecasts of $\dot{W}_t$ and $P\dot{N}FD_t$ at Quarterly Percentage Rates for Medium High Unemployment Assumption

	DLA Controls Model		ILA Controls Model		CPA Controls Model	
$ESP_t = 0$	$\dot{W}_t$	$P\dot{N}FD_t$	$\dot{W}_t$	$P\dot{N}FD_t$	$\dot{W}_t$	$P\dot{N}FD_t$
73:1	2.35	1.06	0.90	0.62	−0.11	−1.08
73:2	1.40	0.95	1.36	0.74	0.92	0.57
73:3	1.54	0.91	1.28	0.75	1.48	0.91
73:4	1.63	0.93	1.13	0.71	1.73	1.12
74:1	1.93	1.09	1.15	0.66	1.68	1.02
74:2	1.76	1.02	1.15	0.62	1.74	1.06
74:3	1.82	0.98	1.16	0.59	1.84	1.11
74:4	1.87	0.96	1.15	0.57	2.02	1.22
$ESP_t = 0.5$	$\dot{W}_t$	$P\dot{N}FD_t$	$\dot{W}_t$	$P\dot{N}FD_t$	$\dot{W}_t$	$P\dot{N}FD_t$
73:1	2.27	0.79	1.02	0.46	−0.14	−1.24
73:2	1.29	0.67	1.47	0.58	0.86	0.38
73:3	1.38	0.61	1.39	0.59	1.42	0.72
73:4	1.44	0.62	1.22	0.55	1.68	0.92
74:1	1.71	0.77	1.25	0.51	1.62	0.82
74:2	1.49	0.68	1.25	0.47	1.68	0.85
74:3	1.52	0.61	1.26	0.44	1.77	0.89
74:4	1.55	0.58	1.26	0.42	1.97	1.03
$ESP_t = 1.0$	$\dot{W}_t$	$P\dot{N}FD_t$	$\dot{W}_t$	$P\dot{N}FD_t$	$\dot{W}_t$	$P\dot{N}FD_t$
73:1	2.18	0.53	1.15	0.29	−0.16	−1.42
73:2	1.17	0.39	1.58	0.42	0.81	0.18
73:3	1.23	0.31	1.49	0.44	1.37	0.52
73:4	1.25	0.31	1.32	0.40	1.63	0.73
74:1	1.48	0.45	1.35	0.37	1.57	0.62
74:2	1.23	0.34	1.36	0.32	1.61	0.65
74:3	1.22	0.25	1.36	0.29	1.71	0.69
74:4	1.22	0.19	1.36	0.27	1.92	0.84

Source: Authors' estimates.

these models, the following answers can be given to the three questions posed in
Chapter 1. First, the simulations of the historical models under the assumptions
of an economy with no controls indicate that inflation showed no signs of
slowing down at the time controls were imposed. All three models predict rapid
advances in wages and prices over the six quarters beginning with 1971:3. This
finding provides at least prima facie evidence that a controls program was
necessary to stem the unrestrained rise of wages and prices.

Second, our models unanimously indicate that at least while in effect the
controls did moderate the rate of inflation in prices. They lead to mixed

Table 7-3

Forecasts of $\dot{W}_t$ and $\dot{PNFD}_t$ at Quarterly Percentage Rates for Medium Low Unemployment Assumption

	DLA Controls Model		ILA Controls Model		CPA Controls Model	
$ESP_t = 0$	$\dot{W}_t$	$\dot{PNFD}_t$	$\dot{W}_t$	$\dot{PNFD}_t$	$\dot{W}_t$	$\dot{PNFD}_t$
73:1	2.35	1.07	0.91	0.61	−0.10	−1.07
73:2	1.46	0.96	1.38	0.75	0.96	0.60
73:3	1.57	0.92	1.31	0.76	1.54	0.95
73:4	1.67	0.94	1.18	0.72	1.79	1.16
74:1	1.99	1.12	1.21	0.68	1.73	1.05
74:2	1.61	1.04	1.22	0.65	1.77	1.08
74:3	1.87	0.99	1.22	0.62	1.84	1.11
74:4	1.93	0.98	1.21	0.59	2.01	1.23
$ESP_t = 0.5$	$\dot{W}_t$	$\dot{PNFD}_t$	$\dot{W}_t$	$\dot{PNFD}_t$	$\dot{W}_t$	$\dot{PNFD}_t$
73:1	2.27	0.80	1.03	0.46	−0.13	−1.24
73:2	1.30	0.67	1.49	0.59	0.91	0.41
73:3	1.41	0.62	1.42	0.60	1.48	0.75
73:4	1.42	0.64	1.26	0.57	1.74	0.96
74:1	1.76	0.79	1.31	0.54	1.68	0.86
74:2	1.55	0.70	1.31	0.49	1.70	0.87
74:3	1.57	0.64	1.31	0.47	1.78	0.90
74:4	1.60	0.60	1.31	0.44	1.97	1.03
$ESP_t = 1.0$	$\dot{W}_t$	$\dot{PNFD}_t$	$\dot{W}_t$	$\dot{PNFD}_t$	$\dot{W}_t$	$\dot{PNFD}_t$
73:1	2.19	0.54	1.15	0.30	−0.15	−1.42
73:2	1.19	0.39	1.59	0.43	0.86	0.22
73:3	1.26	0.32	1.52	0.45	1.43	0.56
73:4	1.29	0.32	1.37	0.42	1.69	0.77
74:1	1.54	0.47	1.41	0.39	1.63	0.66
74:2	1.29	0.36	1.41	0.35	1.64	0.67
74:3	−1.27	0.27	1.41	0.32	1.71	0.69
74:4	1.27	0.22	1.41	0.29	1.92	0.84

Source: Authors' estimates.

conclusions regarding the impact on wages, however, with the DLA model suggesting a downward impact at least in the short run and the ILA and CPA models suggesting an upward one.

Third, all of the models indicate that controls helped shift the long run Phillips curve toward the origin. Several studies have shown a worsening of the unemployment-inflation tradeoff over the last decade.[2] Our findings indicate that controls have not only stopped, but have reversed this rightward movement of the long run Phillips curve by slowing the inflation process. Whether this phenomenon is temporary or permanent cannot be ascertained at this early date.

Several comments on these finding are in order. Our analysis does most

Table 7-4

Forecasts of $\dot{W}_t$ and $\dot{PNFD}_t$ at Quarterly Percentage Rates for Low Unemployment Assumption

	DLA Controls Model		ILA Controls Model		CPA Controls Model	
$ESP_t = 0$	$\dot{W}_t$	$\dot{PNFD}_t$	$\dot{W}_t$	$\dot{PNFD}_t$	$\dot{W}_t$	$\dot{PNFD}_t$
73:1	2.36	1.07	0.91	0.62	−0.10	−0.11
73:2	1.42	0.96	1.38	0.75	0.96	0.60
73:3	1.58	0.92	1.33	0.76	1.57	0.98
73:4	1.70	0.95	1.21	0.73	1.85	1.19
74:1	2.02	1.13	1.25	0.70	1.77	1.08
74:2	1.86	1.06	1.28	0.67	1.83	1.12
74:3	1.96	1.03	1.32	0.65	1.97	1.19
74:4	2.02	1.02	1.32	0.64	2.09	1.27
$ESP_t = 0.5$	$\dot{W}_t$	$\dot{PNFD}_t$	$\dot{W}_t$	$\dot{PNFD}_t$	$\dot{W}_t$	$\dot{PNFD}_t$
73:1	2.27	0.80	1.03	0.46	−0.13	−1.24
73:2	1.30	0.67	1.49	0.59	0.91	0.41
73:3	1.43	0.62	1.43	0.61	1.52	0.78
73:4	1.51	0.64	1.30	0.58	1.80	1.00
74:1	1.79	0.80	1.34	0.55	1.71	0.88
74:2	1.60	0.72	1.36	0.51	1.76	0.91
74:3	1.66	0.66	1.40	0.50	1.89	0.99
74:4	1.69	0.64	1.40	0.48	2.03	1.08
$ESP_t = 1.0$	$\dot{W}_t$	$\dot{PNFD}_t$	$\dot{W}_t$	$\dot{PNFD}_t$	$\dot{W}_t$	$\dot{PNFD}_t$
73:1	2.19	0.54	1.15	0.30	−0.15	−1.42
73:2	1.19	0.39	1.59	0.43	0.85	0.22
73:3	1.27	0.33	1.54	0.45	1.46	0.58
73:4	1.32	0.34	1.40	0.43	1.75	0.81
74:1	1.57	0.48	1.44	0.40	1.66	0.68
74:2	1.34	0.37	1.47	0.37	1.69	0.71
74:3	1.36	0.30	1.50	0.35	1.83	0.78
74:4	1.37	0.25	1.51	0.33	1.99	0.88

Source: Authors' estimates.

definitely not imply that the actions of the Pay Board and the Price Commission were directly responsible for the impact on inflation we have found. Indeed, others have concluded that the restraint appears to have come from the changed environment in which price and wage mechanisms operate rather than direct regulatory effects.[3] That we found the influence of Phase II on wages to have been ambiguous could be attributable in part to Pay Board decisions to permit retroactive implementation of wage increases and to qualify the 5.5 percent wage standard with catch-up and other escape clauses.[4]

Organized labor has maintained since the start of Phase II, and others outside its ranks have concurred, that controls have redistributed income away from labor to profits by clamping down on wages while letting prices continue to rise.[5] Our analysis contradicts such an assessment, for it implies that Phase II has favored, not penalized labor in this regard.[e] First, the direct effects on wages and prices measured by the equations in Table 6-2 indicate the freeze and Phase II increased the rate of growth of real wages. Each of the controls versions of our three models shows that prices were held down by controls, while wages were either pushed up or held down to a lesser extent. Second, while the total impacts on wages and prices implied by the simulation analyses and the long run Phillips curves differ among our three models, all of these total impact estimates indicate a redistribution of income towards workers in the form of higher real incomes. As reported in Table 6-7, on the average our simulations of the DLA, ILA, and CPA models for the 1971:3 to 1972:4 period indicate that prices were held down overall by approximately 1.38 percentage points more per annum than wages were.

---

[e]It is possible that Phase II redistributed income away from labor to profits by encouraging the substitution of capital for labor, but we abstract from this point, since that is not the argument which organized labor has made. For similar reasons, we also abstract from the possibility that nonunion workers have received all the income redistribution spoils, leaving union workers worse off.

Appendix A
Definition of Variables

In the following list t subscripts are used to denote quarter-year time periods, as in the body of the text. The L subscripts placed on variables in the body of the text to indicate their use in an Almon distributed lag are omitted, however, See Table 2-1 in Chapter 2 for an explanation of these latter subscripts. Variables whose definitions do not appear in the following list are data series used only to construct other variables, but are not themselves used in the analysis. These data series are described in Appendix B.

1. $W_t = \left(WAGE_t\right)\left(\dfrac{WSS_t}{WS_t}\right)$

2. $\dot{W}_t = \dfrac{W_t - W_{t-1}}{W_{t-1}}$

3. $\overline{\dot{W}}_t = 0.4\,\dot{W}_t + 0.3\,\dot{W}_{t-1} + 0.2\,\dot{W}_{t-2} + 0.1\,\dot{W}_{t-3}$

4. $\left(\dfrac{\dot{W}}{Q^*}\right)_t = \dfrac{\dfrac{W_t}{Q_t^*} - \dfrac{W_{t-1}}{Q_{t-1}^*}}{\dfrac{W_{t-1}}{Q_{t-1}^*}}$

5. $\dot{CMH}_t = \dfrac{CMH_t - CMH_{t-1}}{CMH_{t-1}}$

6. $\overline{\dot{CMH}}_t = 0.4\,\dot{CMH}_t + 0.3\,\dot{CMH}_{t-1} + 0.2\,\dot{CMH}_{t-2} + 0.1\,\dot{CMH}_{t-3}$

7. $(\overline{\dot{W}}_t - \overline{\dot{CMH}}_t) = \overline{\dot{W}}_t - \overline{\dot{CMH}}_t$

8. $\left(\dfrac{\dot{W}}{CMH}\right)_t' = 0.25\left(\dfrac{\dfrac{W_t}{CMH_t} - \dfrac{W_{t-4}}{CMH_{t-4}}}{\dfrac{W_{t-4}}{CMH_{t-4}}}\right)$

9. $\left(\dfrac{CMH}{W}\right)'_t = 0.25 \left(\dfrac{\dfrac{CMH_t}{W_t} - \dfrac{CMH_{t-4}}{W_{t-4}}}{\dfrac{CMH_{t-4}}{W_{t-4}}} \right)$

10. $\dot{PCD}_t = \dfrac{PCD_t - PCD_{t-1}}{PCD_{t-1}}$

11. $\overline{\dot{PCD}}_t = 0.4\,\dot{PCD}_t + 0.3\,\dot{PCD}_{t-1} + 0.2\,\dot{PCD}_{t-2} + 0.1\,\dot{PCD}_{t-3}$

12. $\dot{PNFD}_t = \dfrac{PNFD_t - PNFD_{t-1}}{PNFD_{t-1}}$

13. $(\dot{PNFD}_t - \dot{PCD}_t) = \dot{PNFD}_t - \dot{PCD}_t$

14. $\dot{JP}_t = \left\{ (\dot{PCD}_t + \ldots + \dot{PCD}_{t-7}) - 0.05 \right\}$ or zero, whichever is algebraically larger

15. $\dot{RMP}_t = \dfrac{RMP_t - RMP_{t-1}}{RMP_{t-1}}$

16. $\dot{Q}_t = \dfrac{Q_t - Q_{t-1}}{Q_{t-1}}$

17. $\overline{\dot{Q}}_t = 0.4\,\dot{Q}_t + 0.3\,\dot{Q}_{t-1} + 0.2\,\dot{Q}_{t-2} + 0.1\,\dot{Q}_{t-3}$

18. $Q_t^* = e^{-0.56 + 0.0066\,\text{Time}}$, where Time has the value 1 in 1947:1 and increases by 1 each quarter-year period thereafter. The coefficients -0.56 and 0.0066 are based on regression of $\ln(Q_t)$ against Time. Thus, Q_t^* can be interpreted as the trend value of Q_t. Regressions for the intervals 1948:4 to 1969:4, 1954:3 to 1970:4, and 1955:1 to 1971:2 all yielded approximately the same coefficients.

19. $\dot{Q}_t^* = \dfrac{Q_t^* - \dot{Q}_{t-1}^*}{Q_{t-1}^*}$

20. $\left(\dfrac{\dot{Q}}{Q^*}\right)_t = \dfrac{\dfrac{Q_t}{Q^*_t} - \dfrac{Q_{t-1}}{Q^*_{t-1}}}{\dfrac{Q_{t-1}}{Q^*_{t-1}}}$

21. $A\dot{V}P_t = \dfrac{(PNFD_t)(Q_t) - (PNFD_{t-1})(Q_{t-1})}{(PNFD_{t-1})(Q_{t-1})}$

22. $\left(\dfrac{1}{U}\right)_t = \dfrac{1}{U_t}$

23. $\dot{U}_t = \dfrac{U_t - U_{t-1}}{U_{t-1}}$

24. DU_t, or unemployment dispersion, measures the dispersion of unemployment rates weighted by wage rates and hours worked among sectors of the labor force delineated by age and sex. See Appendix B.

25. UD_t, or disguised unemployment, equals the labor reserve, defined as the potential total labor force (including the armed forces) minus the actual total labor force, divided by the civilian labor force. The potential total labor force, defined as the population times its potential total labor force participation rate, is computed separately for "primary" male workers aged 25-54 and "secondary" workers. See Appendix B.

26. UH_t, or unemployment of hours, equal 1.0 minus the ratio of actual to potential hours worked in the private, nonfarm economy. See Appendix B.

27. $E_t = \dfrac{TP_t + 0.5\, TW_t}{YP_t}$

28. $T(E)_t = \dfrac{1}{1 - E_t}$

30. $\overline{\dot{T(E)}'_t} = 10\, \dot{T(E)}_t - 4.5\, \dot{T(E)}_{t-1} - 3.0\, \dot{T(E)}_{t-2} - 1.5\, \dot{T(E)}_{t-3}$

29. $\dot{T(E)}_t = \dfrac{T(E)_t - T(E)_{t-1}}{T(E)_{t-1}}$

31. $F_t = \dfrac{0.5\,TW_t}{YP_t}$

32. $T(F)_t = \dfrac{1}{1 - F_t}$

33. $T(\dot{F})_t = \dfrac{T(F)_t - T(F)_{t-1}}{T(F)_{t-1}}$

34. $T(\dot{F})'_t = T(\dot{F})_t - 0.5\,T(\dot{F})_{t-1} - 0.33\,T(\dot{F})_{t-2} - 0.17\,T(\dot{F})_{t-3}$

35. $\dot{C}_t = \dfrac{C_t - C_{t-1}}{C_{t-1}}$

36. $UFK_t = \dfrac{\dfrac{UFD_t}{PD_t} + \dfrac{UFND_t}{PND_t}}{K_t}$

37. $(UFK_t - UFK_{t-1})' = UFK_t - UFK_{t-1}$ or zero, whichever is algebraically larger.

38. $UFK^*_t = e^{0.113938 - 0.00782579\ \text{Time}}$, where Time has the value 1 in 1947:1 and increases by one each quarter-year period thereafter. The coefficients 0.113938 and 0.00782579 are based on regressions of ln (UFK_t) against Time over the interval 1948:4 to 1969:4. Thus, UFK^*_t can be interpreted as the trend value of UFK_t. The coefficient estimates displayed a good deal of instability when alternative estimation intervals were tested.

39. $\left(\dfrac{U\dot{F}K}{UFK^*}\right)_t = \dfrac{\dfrac{UFK_t}{UFK^*_t} - \dfrac{UFK_{t-1}}{UFK^*_{t-1}}}{\dfrac{UFK_{t-1}}{UFK^*_{t-1}}}$

40. $UF_t = UFD_t + UFND_t$

41. $\left(\dfrac{U\dot{F}_t - UF_{t-1}}{S_t}\right) = \dfrac{UF_t - UF_{t-1}}{S_t}$

42. $\dot{CUR}_t = \dfrac{CUR_t - CUR_{t-1}}{CUR_{t-1}}$

43. GP_t, the mid-1960s wage and price guidelines dummy, has the values 0.25 in 1962:1 and 1967:3, 0.50 in 1962:2 and 1967:2, 0.75 in 1962:3 and 1967:1, 1.0 from 1962:4 through 1966:4, and 0.0 in all other quarter-year periods.

44. ESP_t, the 90-day freeze and Phase II dummy, is zero for all quarter-year periods up through 1971:2 and one for all of them thereafter.

Appendix B
Sources of Data

All data series appearing in the following list were obtained from the Data Resources, Inc. computer based data bank unless explicitly noted to the contrary. The following abbreviations are used throughout the list: BLS for U.S. Department of Labor, Bureau of Labor Statistics; BEA for U.S. Department of Commerce, Bureau of Economic Analysis (formerly Office of Business Economics); NIPA for National Income Accounts of the United States; Census for U.S. Department of Commerce, Bureau of the Census; FRB for Board of Governors, Federal Reserve System. All monthly series were transformed into quarterly ones by averaging their values for the three months of each quarter, excepting S for which the sum of the monthly values was used.

1. $WAGE_t$
   (a) Beginning in 1964, BLS seasonally adjusted monthly index of average hourly earnings of production workers in the private, nonfarm economy, adjusted for interindustry employment shifts and manufacturing overtime, with index base = 1.0 in 1967.
   (b) Prior to 1964, Robert J. Gordon quarterly index of adjusted average hourly earnings of employees in the private, nonfarm economy, adjusted for interindustry employment shifts, multiplied by the 1964:1 ratio of the series above to this series. Obtained from Robert J. Gordon.[1]

2. WSS_t

   BEA seasonally adjusted compensation of employees in billions of current dollars, computed quarterly at annual rates as part of the NIPA.

3. WS_t

   BEA seasonally adjusted wages and salaries in billions of current dollars, computed quarterly at annual rates as part of the NIPA.

4. CMH_t

   BLS seasonally adjusted quarterly index of compensation per manhour in the private, nonfarm economy, with index base = 1.0 in 1967.

5. PCD_t

   BEA seasonally adjusted GNP implicit price deflator for personal consumption expenditure, with index base = 1.0 in 1958, computed quarterly as part of the NIPA.

6. $PNFD_t$

BEA seasonally adjusted price of gross product (GNP implicit price deflator) for nonfarm industries, with index base = 1.0 in 1958, computed quarterly as part of the NIPA.[a]

7. RMP_t

BLS nonseasonally adjusted monthly index of wholesale prices for raw industrial commodities, with index base = 1.0 in 1967.

8. Q_t

BLS seasonally adjusted quarterly index of output per manhour in the private, nonfarm economy, with index base = 1.0 in 1967.

9. U_t

BLS seasonally adjusted unemployment rate for all civilian workers, currently published monthly in *Employment and Earnings*.[b]

10. DU_t

Unemployment dispersion as described in Appendix A. Obtained from George L. Perry.[2]

11. UD_t

Disguised unemployment as described in Appendix A. Obtained from Robert J. Gordon.[3]

12. UH_t

Unemployment of hours as described in Appendix A. Obtained from Robert J. Gordon.[4]

13. TP_t

BEA seasonally adjusted personal tax and nontax payments in billions of current dollars, computed quarterly at annual rates as part of the NIPA.

14. TW_t

BEA seasonally adjusted contributions for social insurance in billions of current dollars, computed quarterly at annual rates as part of the NIPA.

15. YP_t

BEA seasonally adjusted personal income in billions of current dollars, computed quarterly at annual rates as part of the NIPA.

---

[a]According to Data Resources, Inc., the price of gross product for the private, nonfarm economy is the same thing as the GNP implicit price deflator for that sector.

[b]We have used U in decimal form, not in percentage form.

16. C_t

BEA seasonally adjusted corporate profits before taxes excluding inventory valuation adjustment in billions of current dollars, computed quarterly at annual rates as part of the NIPA.

17. UFD_t

Census seasonally adjusted monthly series on unfilled orders in durable manufacturing at month end in billions of current dollars, currently published in *Manufacturers Shipments, Inventories, and Orders* as Series M3-1 and Historical Supplements Thereto.

18. $UFND_t$

Census seasonally adjusted monthly series on unfilled orders in nondurable manufacturing at month end in billions of current dollars, currently published in *Manufacturers Shipments, Inventories, and Orders* as Series M3-1 and Historical Supplements Thereto.

19. PD_t

BEA seasonally adjusted GNP implicit price deflator for durable goods output, with index base = 1.0 in 1958, computed quarterly as part of the NIPA.

20. PND_t

BEA seasonally adjusted GNP implicit price deflator for nondurable goods output, with index base = 1.0 in 1958, computed quarterly as part of the NIPA.

21. K_t

FRB quarterly series on physical capacity in manufacturing.

22. S_t

BEA seasonally adjusted monthly series on sales in manufacturing and trade in billions of current dollars at monthly rates, published monthly in *Survey of Current Business.*

23. CUR_t

FRB seasonally adjusted quarterly series on capacity utilization rate in manufacturing, published in *Federal Reserve Bulletin* and *Statistical Release E.5.*

24. GP_t

Mid-1960s wage-price guidelines dummy variable constructed by the authors as described in Appendix A.

25. ESP_t

90-day wage-price freeze and Phase II dummy variable constructed by the authors as described in Appendix A.

26. GNP_t

BEA seasonally adjusted gross national product in billions of current dollars, computed quarterly at annual rates as part of the NIPA.

27. RUF_t

Seasonally adjusted quarterly series on unfilled orders in manufacturing at month end in billions of 1958 dollars. Obtained from DRI Quarterly Econometric Model.

Appendix C
Correlation Matrices for Wage
and Price Equations

Appendix C
Correlation Matrices for Wage and Price Equations

1. Correlation Matrix for DLA wage Equations (2.3) and (2.4):

	$\left(\dfrac{\dot{w}}{Q}\right)_t$	$\left(\dfrac{1}{U}\right)_t$	DU_t	UD_t	UH_t
$\left(\dfrac{\dot{w}}{Q}\right)_t$	1.000				
$\left(\dfrac{1}{U}\right)_t$	0.466	1.000			
DU_t	0.570	0.714	1.000		
UD_t	-0.591	-0.399	-0.240	1.000	
UH_t	-0.039	-0.578	-0.491	-0.220	1.000
$\dot{PCD}_t$	0.696	0.530	0.641	-0.581	0.008
$(P\dot{N}FD-\dot{PCD})_t$	0.099	0.094	0.034	-0.291	-0.177
$(P\dot{N}FD-\dot{PCD})_{t-1}$	0.225	0.148	-0.010	-0.163	-0.130
$T(\dot{E})_t$	0.126	0.321	0.051	0.094	-0.306
$T(\dot{F})'_t$	0.318	-0.011	-0.042	0.104	-0.053

1. Correlation Matrix for DLA wage Equations (2.3) and (2.4) continued

	$\dot{PCD}_t$	$(\dot{PNFD}-\dot{PCD})_t$	$(\dot{PNFD}-\dot{PCD})_{t-1}$	$T(\dot{E})_t$	$T(F)'_t$
$\left(\dfrac{\dot{W}}{Q}\right)_t$					
$\left(\dfrac{1}{U}\right)_t$					
DU_t					
UD_t					
UH_t					
$\dot{PCD}_t$	1.000				
$(\dot{PNFD}-\dot{PCD})_t$	−0.198	1.000			
$(\dot{PNFD}-\dot{PCD})_{t-1}$	0.042	0.171	1.000		
$T(\dot{E})_t$	0.032	0.053	0.092	1.000	
$T(F)'_t$	−0.017	−0.047	0.238	0.289	1.000

2. Correlation matrix for DLA price Equation (2.5):

	$P\dot{N}FD_t$	$\left(\dfrac{\dot{w}}{Q^*}\right)_t$	$\left(\dfrac{\dot{Q}}{Q^*}\right)_t$	$\left(\dfrac{\dot{w}}{CMH}\right)'_t$	$\left(\dfrac{U\dot{F}K}{UFK^*}\right)_t$
$P\dot{N}FD_t$	1.000				
$\left(\dfrac{\dot{w}}{Q^*}\right)_t$	0.695	1.000			
$\left(\dfrac{\dot{Q}}{Q^*}\right)_t$	−0.411	−0.017	1.000		
$\left(\dfrac{\dot{w}}{CMH}\right)'_t$	−0.112	0.075	0.067	1.000	
$\left(\dfrac{U\dot{F}K}{UFK^*}\right)_t$	−0.161	−0.231	0.100	−0.257	1.000

3. Correlation matrix for ILA wage Equation (3.3):

	$\dot{w}_t$	$\left(\frac{1}{U}\right)_t$	$\overline{PCD}_t$	$\dot{JP}_t$	$\overline{T(E)}_t$	GP_t
$\dot{w}_t$	1.000					
$\left(\frac{1}{U}\right)_t$	0.467	1.000				
$\overline{PCD}_t$	0.719	0.478	1.000			
$\dot{JP}_t$	0.679	0.116	0.798	1.000		
$\overline{T(E)}'_t$	0.135	−0.005	−0.141	−0.125	1.000	
GP_t	−0.414	0.006	−0.328	−0.355	−0.004	1.000

4. Correlation matrix for ILA price Equation (3.4):

	$P\dot{N}FD_t$	$(\dot{\bar{W}}_{t-1} - 0.0065)$	$(\dot{w}_t - \dot{w}_{t-1})$	$(\dot{\bar{Q}}_{t-1} - 0.0065)$	$(\dot{Q}_t - \dot{\bar{Q}}_{t-1})$	$(\dot{\bar{W}}_t - \dot{\overline{CMH}}_t)$	$(UFK_t - UFK_{t-1})'$
$P\dot{N}FD_t$	1.000						
$(\dot{\bar{W}}_{t-1} - 0.0065)$	0.767	1.000					
$(\dot{w}_t - \dot{w}_{t-1})$	0.101	-0.125	1.000				
$(\dot{\bar{Q}}_{t-1} - 0.0065)$	-0.323	-0.385	0.026	1.000			
$(\dot{Q}_t - \dot{\bar{Q}}_{t-1})$	-0.196	-0.051	0.255	-0.487	1.000		
$(\dot{\bar{W}}_t - \dot{\overline{CMH}}_t)$	-0.043	0.180	0.037	-0.183	0.067	1.000	
$(UFK_t - UFK_{t-1})'$	-0.063	-0.322	0.127	0.408	-0.333	-0.131	1.000

5. Correlation matrix for CPA wage Equation (4.4):

	$\dot{w}_t$	$\left(\frac{1}{U}\right)_t$	$\dot{U}_t$	$P\dot{C}D_t$	$P\dot{N}FD_t$	$\dot{Q}_t$	$\dot{C}_t$	$\dot{w}_{t-1}$
$\dot{w}_t$	1.000							
$\left(\frac{1}{U}\right)_t$	0.467	1.000						
$\dot{U}_t$	0.031	−0.190	1.000					
$P\dot{C}D_t$	0.696	0.530	0.340	1.000				
$P\dot{N}FD_t$	0.695	0.541	0.198	0.782	1.000			
$\dot{Q}_t$	−0.017	−0.304	−0.301	−0.359	−0.411	1.000		
$\dot{C}_t$	0.056	−0.207	−0.588	−0.399	−0.228	0.665	1.000	
$\dot{w}_{t-1}$	0.633	0.411	0.249	0.668	0.657	−0.305	−0.209	1.000

6. Correlation matrix for CPA price Equation (4.4):

	$PN\dot{F}D_t$	$\dot{w}_t$	$\dot{Q}_t$	$R\dot{M}P_t$	$C\ddot{U}R_t$	$\left(\dfrac{UF_t - UF_{t-1}}{S_t}\right)$
$PN\dot{F}D_t$	1.000					
$\dot{w}_t$	0.695	1.000				
$\dot{Q}_t$	-0.411	-0.017	1.000			
$R\dot{M}P_t$	-0.010	-0.033	-0.032	1.000		
$C\ddot{U}R_t$	-0.287	-0.071	0.550	0.371	1.000	
$\left(\dfrac{UF_t - UF_{t-1}}{S_t}\right)$	0.041	-0.085	0.032	0.403	0.513	1.000

Appendix D
Preliminary Estimates of Alternative
CPA Wage and Price Equations

Table D-1. Coefficient Estimates and Summary Statistics for the Preliminary CPA Wage Equation Regressions (with t-statistics in parentheses)

Equation Number	Intercept	$\left(\frac{1}{U}\right)_t$	$\dot{U}_t$	$P\dot{C}D_t$	$PN\dot{F}D_t$	$\dot{Q}_t$	$A\dot{V}P_t$	C_t	$\dot{w}_{t-1}$	$\dot{w}_{t-2}$	$\bar{R}^2$	S.E.	D.W.
1	0.0058 (2.76)	−0.0000 (−0.21)	−0.0119 (−1.86)	0.8299 (5.61)				0.0000 (0.99)			0.509	0.00296	1.61
2	0.0045 (2.17)	−0.0000 (−0.33)	−0.0131 (−2.27)	0.6495 (4.15)				0.0000 (0.053)	0.3031 (2.66)		0.554	0.00282	2.10
3	0.0037 (1.71)	−0.0000 (−0.35)	−0.0136 (−2.35)	0.5621 (3.18)				0.0000 (0.53)	0.2732 (2.33)	0.1458 (1.06)	0.555	0.00282	2.06
4	0.0032 (1.56)	0.0001 (0.76)	−0.0058 (−1.02)	0.7587 (5.52)			0.1654 (3.48)	0.0000 (0.30)			0.585	0.00272	1.59
5	0.0019 (0.096)	0.0001 (0.69)	−0.0078 (−1.42)	0.5784 (4.03)			0.1654 (3.69)	−0.0000 (−0.21)	0.3030 (2.93)		0.631	0.00257	2.10
6	0.0016 (0.077)	0.0001 (0.65)	−0.0081 (−1.47)	0.5377 (3.32)			0.1612 (3.52)	−0.0000 (−0.20)	0.2884 (2.69)	0.0710 (0.56)	0.627	0.00258	2.07
7	0.0038 (1.73)	0.0001 (0.60)	−0.0075 (−1.24)	0.8702 (6.06)		0.1176 (2.37)		0.0000 (0.47)			0.544	0.00286	1.51
8	0.0021 (0.99)	0.0001 (0.63)	−0.0091 (−1.61)	0.6768 (4.56)		0.1318 (2.82)		−0.0000 (−0.13)	0.3333 (3.08)		0.600	0.00267	2.05
9	0.0015 (0.69)	0.0001 (0.59)	−0.0096 (−1.70)	0.6025 (3.58)		0.1290 (2.76)		−0.0000 (−0.12)	0.3075 (2.75)	0.1229 (0.94)	0.600	0.00268	2.01
10	0.0064 (3.16)	−0.0001 (−0.77)	−0.0110 (−1.92)	0.5331 (2.98)	0.3845 (2.68)			0.0000 (1.19)			0.555	0.00282	1.85

Table D-2 continued

Equation Number	Intercept	$\left(\frac{1}{U}\right)_t$	$\dot{U}_t$	$P\dot{C}D_t$	$P\dot{N}FD_t$	$\dot{Q}_t$	$A\dot{V}P_t$	C_t	$\dot{w}_{t-1}$	$\dot{w}_{t-2}$	$\bar{R}^2$	S.E.	D.W.
11	0.5246 (2.56)	-0.0001 (-0.74)	-0.0125 (-2.22)	0.4600 (2.58)	0.2986 (2.04)			0.000 (0.72)	0.2343 (2.02)		0.576	0.00275	2.16
12	0.0048 (2.17)	-0.0001 (-0.72)	-0.0128 (-2.24)	0.4340 (2.31)	0.2758 (1.78)			0.0000 (0.70)	0.2257 (1.91)	0.0675 (0.48)	0.571	0.00277	2.14
13	0.0041 (1.91)	0.0001 (0.89)	-0.0079 (-1.34)	0.8937 (6.68)		0.1228 (2.56)					0.550	0.00284	1.53
14	0.0021 (0.99)	0.0001 (0.99)	-0.0090 (-1.63)	0.6726 (4.69)		0.1304 (2.90)			0.3306 (3.14)		0.607	0.00265	2.05
15	0.0015 (0.69)	0.0001 (0.60)	-0.0095 (-1.72)	0.5985 (3.67)		0.1277 (2.83)			0.3049 (2.80)	0.1231 (0.95)	0.606	0.00265	2.00
—	0.0040 (1.96)	0.0000 (0.20)	-0.0062 (-1.12)	0.5165 (3.10)	0.4726 (3.47)	0.1500 (3.22)		0.0000 (0.46)			0.615	0.00262	1.83
—	0.0027 (1.31)	0.0000 (0.28)	-0.0077 (-1.43)	0.4380 (2.67)	0.3837 (2.81)	0.1546 (3.44)		-0.0000 (-0.02)	0.2501 (2.34)		0.642	0.00253	2.17
—	0.0026 (1.21)	0.0000 (0.28)	-0.0077 (-1.41)	0.4339 (2.51)	0.3798 (2.60)	0.1541 (3.37)		-0.0000 (-0.02)	0.2487 (2.28)	0.0107 (0.08)	0.636	0.00255	2.16

Source: Authors' estimates.

Note: Equation numbers correspond to those used by Siebert and Zaidi in Table 1 of [42, p. 283]. $A\dot{V}P_t$ is the one-quarter rate of change in value productivity; it is defined in Appendix A. The modified, final version of the CPA wage equation incorporates data revisions made after these preliminary regressions were run.

Table D-2
Coefficient Estimates and Summary Statistics for the Preliminary CPA Price Equation Regressions (with t-statistics in parentheses)

Equation Number	Intercept	$\dot{w}_t$	$\dot{Q}_t$	$R\dot{M}P_t$	$R\dot{M}P_{t-1}$	$C\dot{U}R_t$	$\left(\dfrac{UF_t - UF_{t-1}}{S_t}\right)$	$\bar{R}^2$	S.E.	D.W.
1	−0.0019 (−1.75)	0.6633 (7.67)		0.0017 (0.15)				0.466	0.00295	1.75
2	−0.0019 (−1.74)	0.6634 (7.61)		0.0019 (0.15)	−0.0005 (−0.04)			0.458	0.00297	1.75
3	−0.0007 (−0.69)	0.6654 (8.93)	−0.1885 (−5.05)	0.0002 (0.02)				0.616	0.00250	1.89
4	−0.0018 (−1.76)	0.6475 (7.95)		0.0143 (1.28)		−0.0454 (−3.07)		0.529	0.00277	1.74
5	−0.0021 (−2.18)	0.6598 (8.52)		0.0065 (0.57)		−0.0636 (−4.11)	0.0949 (2.79)	0.576	0.00263	1.94
—	−0.0007 (−0.74)	0.6533 (8.83)	−0.1761 (−3.74)	0.0025 (0.22)		−0.0074 (−0.44)		0.611	0.00252	1.88
—	−0.0011 (−1.14)	0.6608 (9.11)	−0.1485 (−3.08)	−0.0012 (−0.11)		−0.0257 (−1.35)	0.0645 (1.94)	0.628	0.00246	1.96
—	−0.0011 (−1.14)	0.6607 (9.02)	−0.1483 (−2.98)	−0.0013 (−0.11)	0.0003 (0.02)	−0.0259 (−1.27)	0.0645 (1.91)	0.621	0.00248	1.96

Source: Authors' estimates.

Note: Equation numbers correspond to those used by Siebert and Zaidi in Table 2 of [28, p. 285]. The modified, final version of the CPA price equation incorporates data revisions made after these preliminary regressions were run.

**Appendix E
Additional Tables Related to
Chapter 6 Evaluation of the
90-day Freeze and Phase II**

Table E-1

Error Measures for the 1955:1 to 1972:4 DLA, ILA, and CPA Historical Models Simulations

	DLA Model Simulation Using Wage Equation (2.4)	ILA Model Simulation	CPA Model Simulation
$\dot{W}_t$			
Mean Error	−0.000573135	0.000528132	0.000439148
Root Mean Square Error	0.00213362	0.00274639	0.0478879
Mean Absolute Error	0.00163819	0.00206065	0.0038627
Theil U Statistic	0.0811349	0.10970323	0.19071966
$P\dot{N}FD_t$			
Mean Error	−0.000699373	−0.000147087	0.0000190456
Root Mean Square Error	0.00276934	0.00221194	0.00377143
Mean Absolute Error	0.00204481	0.00178965	0.00317300
Theil U Statistic	0.191627958	0.15977533	0.13684085

Source: Authors' estimates.

Note: The mean of $\dot{W}_t$ is 0.0122289; the mean of $P\dot{N}FD_t$ is 0.00585343. For a description of the error measures formulae, see the note to Table 2-3.

Table E-2
Error Measures for the 1971:3 to 1972:4 Subset of the 1955:1 to 1972:4 DLA, ILA, and CPA Historical Models Simulations

	DLA Model Simulation Using Wage Equation (2.4)	ILA Model Simulation	CPA Model Simulation
$\dot{w}_t$			
Mean Error	−0.00229454	0.00349612	0.00423191
Root Mean Square Error	0.00353004	0.00501002	0.00532258
Mean Absolute Error	0.00283515	0.00441345	0.00423959
$P\dot{N}FD_t$			
Mean Error	−0.00583846	−0.00261524	−0.00430803
Root Mean Square Error	0.00653842	0.00367837	0.00264879
Mean Absolute Error	0.00513846	0.00303363	0.00239262

Source: Authors' estimates.

Note: The mean of $\dot{w}_t$ is 0.0156177; the mean of $P\dot{N}FD_t$ is 0.00428515. For a description of the error measures formulae, see the note to Table 2-3. We have omitted the Theil U statistics and the regressions of actual on simulated values owing to the shortness of the simulations period.

Table E-3
Individual Distributed Lag Coefficients for Equations (6.1) and (6.2)

Period	Equation (6.1)		Equation (6.2)	
	$P\dot{C}D_{L,t}$	$(P\dot{N}FD - P\dot{C}D)_{L,t-1}$	$\left(\frac{\dot{w}}{w^*}\right)_{L,t}$	$\left(\frac{\dot{Q}}{Q^*}\right)_{L,t}$
t	0.1095 (1.22)		0.3526 (3.97)	−0.1396 (−4.16)
$t-1$	0.1242 (2.50)	0.0442 (0.43)	0.2076 (3.71)	−0.0414 (−1.54)
$t-2$	0.1296 (5.19)	0.0997 (1.38)	0.1242 (2.15)	−0.0223 (−0.89)
$t-3$	0.1279 (6.58)	0.0511 (0.77)	0.0806 (1.69)	−0.0317 (−1.38)
$t-4$	0.1209 (4.86)	−0.0108 (−0.18)	0.0597 (1.06)	−0.0374 (−1.55)
$t-5$	0.1105 (3.84)	−0.0333 (−0.52)	0.0486 (0.77)	−0.0246 (−1.06)
$t-6$	0.0979 (3.32)	−0.0014 (−0.23)	0.0389 (0.76)	0.0032 (0.13)
$t-7$	0.0848 (3.05)	0.0618 (0.92)	0.0267 (0.69)	0.0245 (0.95)
$t-8$	0.0719 (2.89)	0.0953 (1.33)	0.0122 (0.22)	
$t-9$	0.0602 (2.76)		0.0003 (0.00)	
$t-10$	0.0505 (2.58)			
$t-11$	0.0431 (2.33)			
$t-12$	0.0384 (2.11)			
$t-13$	0.0364 (2.03)			
$t-14$	0.0368 (2.15)			
$t-15$	0.0395 (2.48)			

Table E-3 continued

Period	Equation (6.1)		Equation (6.2)	
	$\dot{PCD}_{L,t}$	$(P\dot{NFD}-\dot{PCD})_{L,t-1}$	$\left(\dfrac{\dot{W}}{W^*}\right)_{L,t}$	$\left(\dfrac{\dot{Q}}{Q^*}\right)_{L,t}$
$t-16$	0.0438 (2.97)			
$t-17$	0.0489 (3.49)			
$t-18$	0.0538 (3.34)			
$t-19$	0.0575 (3.05)			
$t-20$	0.0584 (2.73)			
$t-21$	0.0550 (2.46)			
$t-22$	0.0456 (2.26)			
$t-23$	0.0279 (2.10)			
Mean Lag	8.7762	3.4806	1.7877	0.9778
Sum of Coefficients	1.6732 (8.47)	0.3065 (0.95)	0.9515 (6.69)	−0.2694 (−1.83)

Source: Authors' estimates.

Note: All lags are fourth-degree polynomial Almon lags with the lag coefficient constrained to zero in the period immediately preceding in time the far period in the lag. The lagged coefficients of 1.0, −0.50, −0.33, −0.17 on $T(\dot{F})'_t$ are not listed, because they are imposed rather than estimated.

Table E-4

Error Measures for the 1955:1 to 1971:2 Subset of the 1955:1 to 1972:4 DLA, ILA, and CPA Controls Models Simulations

	DLA Controls Model Simulation	ILA Controls Model Simulation	CPA Controls Model Simulation
$\dot{w}_t$			
Mean Error	-0.000470131	0.000162551	0.0000531011
Root Mean Square Error	0.00201537	0.00249842	0.00535580
Mean Absolute Error	0.00158691	0.00184140	0.00364927
Theil U Statistic	0.0789340	0.10073755	0.214415
Regression of actual on simulated values	$\dot{w}_t = -0.000973 + 1.04\,\hat{\dot{w}}_t$ (-1.01) (15.19) $\bar{R}^2 = 0.779$	$\dot{w}_t = -0.000867 + 1.088\,\hat{\dot{w}}_t$ (-0.72) (10.93) $\bar{R}^2 = 0.646$	$\dot{w}_t = 0.0125 - 0.0463\,\hat{\dot{w}}_t$ (6.12) (-0.28) $\bar{R}^2 = 0.014$
$P\dot{N}FD_t$			
Mean Error	-0.000271520	0.000039804	0.0000850922
Root Mean Square Error	0.00202770	0.00204708	0.00427811
Mean Absolute Error	0.00161366	0.00171230	0.00441586
Theil U Statistic	0.141124	0.145748	0.308189
Regression of actual on simulated values	$P\dot{N}FD_t =$ $-0.000280 + 1.001\,P\hat{\dot{N}}FD_t$ (-0.54) (13.79) $\bar{R}^2 = 0.744$	$P\dot{N}FD_t =$ $-0.000117 + 1.02\,P\hat{\dot{N}}FD_t$ (-0.22) (13.47) $\bar{R}^2 = 0.735$	$P\dot{N}FD_t =$ $0.000375 + 0.377\,P\hat{\dot{N}}FD_t$ (3.55) (2.38) $\bar{R}^2 = 0.067$

Source: Authors' estimates.

Note: The mean of $\dot{w}_t$ is 0.0119209; the mean of $P\dot{N}FD_t$ is 0.00599600. For a description of the error measures formulae, see the note to Table 2-3.

Table E-5
Error Measures for the 1971:3 to 1972:4 Subset of the 1955:1 to 1972:4 DLA, ILA, and CPA Controls Models Simulations

	DLA Controls Model Simulation	ILA Controls Model Simulation	CPA Controls Model Simulation
$\dot{w}_t$			
Mean Error	0.00123016	0.00227967	0.00415961
Root Mean Square Error	0.00347226	0.00417453	0.00542059
Mean Absolute Error	0.00258318	0.00358729	0.00425930
$P\dot{N}FD_t$			
Mean Error	0.000519239	0.00107503	0.00272077
Root Mean Square Error	0.00259164	0.00273401	0.00390662
Mean Absolute Error	0.00211419	0.00224030	0.00314829

Source: Authors' estimates.

Note: The mean of $\dot{w}_t$ is 0.0156177; the mean of $P\dot{N}FD_t$ is 0.00428515. For a description of the error measures formulae, see the note to Table 2-3. We have omitted the Theil U statistics and the regressions of actual on simulated values owing to the shortness of the simulations period.

Table E-6

Values of $\dot{W}_t$ and $P\dot{N}FD_t$ Expressed in Percents as Predicted with 1971:3 to 1972:4 DLA, ILA, and CPA Historical and Controls Models Simulations

	Actual	DLA Models		ILA Models		CPA Models	
		Historical	Controls	Historical	Controls	Historical	Controls
$\dot{W}_t$							
71:3	1.58	1.84	1.62	1.68	1.83	1.26	1.31
71:4	1.14	1.88	1.59	1.62	1.69	1.02	1.17
72:1	2.16	2.19	1.87	1.73	1.73	1.14	1.16
72:2	1.44	1.77	1.38	1.23	1.20	1.10	1.08
72:3	1.26	1.80	1.32	1.18	1.10	1.12	1.17
72:4	1.80	1.80	1.25	1.16	1.21	1.19	1.12
$P\dot{N}FD_t$							
71:3	0.59	0.96	0.48	1.02	0.63	0.64	0.36
71:4	0.00	1.14	0.45	0.87	0.47	0.43	0.21
72:1	0.88	1.14	0.55	0.91	0.52	0.47	0.16
72:2	0.29	1.04	0.40	0.74	0.29	0.40	0.07
72:3	0.29	1.02	0.29	0.67	0.22	0.43	0.15
72:4	0.51	1.13	0.37	0.71	0.31	0.52	0.15

Source: Authors' estimates.

Note: The values reported in this table were simulated in decimal form at quarterly rates by the models, but have been restated in percent form at quarterly rates for ease of interpretation.

Appendix F
Data Used to Forecast 1973 and
1974 Wage and Price Changes in
Chapter 7 Simulations

Table F-1

Exogenous Variables Obtained from DRI Model

Date	CMH_t	Q_t	YP_t	TP_t
73:1	1.45515	1.14922	985.88	132.873
73:2	1.47748	1.15917	1004.87	139.042
73:3	1.50035	1.16582	1.024.93	145.372
73:4	1.52258	1.17406	1044.59	147.630
74:1	1.54462	1.18293	1064.08	150.177
74:2	1.56714	1.19637	1083.16	153.185
74:3	1.59001	1.20926	1102.26	156.081
74:4	1.61272	1.22209	1117.63	158.531

Date	TW_t	K_t	RUF_t	GNP_t
73:1	88.206	1.50536	69.8789	1229.0
73:2	90.154	1.52082	72.0610	1253.1
73:3	92.111	1.53624	73.6754	1279.9
73:4	94.105	1.55186	75.7603	1303.5
74:1	98.064	1.56747	77.4000	1330.5
74:2	100.172	1.58361	79.4252	1353.5
74:3	102.305	1.59976	81.1518	1376.0
74:4	104.306	1.61559	82.7724	1397.9

Date	C_t	Medium High Unemployment Rate
73:1	104.9	5.033
73:2	107.4	4.948
73:3	110.0	4.934
73:4	114.6	4.901
74:1	118.7	4.872
74:2	119.3	4.853
74:3	119.1	4.811
74:4	120.5	4.806

Source: DRI Quarterly Econometric Model, Data Resources, Inc., Lexington, Massachusetts.

Table F-2
Exogenous Variables Forecasted by Authors

Date	UF_t	S_t	
73:1	74.604	393.093	
73:2	77.200	400.053	
73:3	79.121	407.793	
73:4	81.602	414.610	
74:1	83.553	422.408	
74:2	85.963	429.050	
74:3	88.017	435.549	
74:4	89.945	441.874	

Date	Low Unemployment Rate	Medium Low Unemployment Rate	High Unemployment Rate
73:1	5.0	5.0	5.2
73:2	4.8	4.8	5.2
73:3	4.6	4.7	5.1
73:4	4.4	4.6	5.1
74:1	4.3	4.5	5.1
74:2	4.2	4.5	5.0
74:3	4.0	4.5	5.0
74:4	4.0	4.5	5.0

Source: Authors' estimates.

Notes

Preface

1. See [4].

Chapter 1
Introduction

1. For a review of several past wage and price studies of the United States and other nations, see [17].

2. See [37]. Although Phillips is generally credited with discovering the tradeoff between inflation and unemployment, Irving Fisher had previously written a little known paper on the same subject; see [16].

3. See [50], [43], and [18].

4. See [29], [32], and [18].

5. See [12], [18], and [47].

6. See [6, p. 351].

7. See [24].

8. See [33] and [34, pp. 27-29, 48-52, 112-114].

9. For econometric evidence on the price setting process, see [13], [22], [41], and [42]. For other evidence on it, see [25] and [26].

10. See [18, pp. 127-130] and [12, pp. 21-22].

11. See [30, p. 258] and [42, p. 281].

12. See [42,]. 282].

13. For a more detailed discussion of this point, see [6, pp. 351-353].

14. For discussions of the Economic Stabilization Program rules and their effectiveness, see [3], [6, pp. 354-376], and [49, pp. 235-270]. The only benefit-cost of the Economic Stabilization Program of which we are aware is [27].

15. For example, see [10, pp. 272-273], [12, p. 8], and [17, pp. 672-673].

Chapter 2
A Distributed Lag Adjustment Model

1. See [18].

2. See [18, pp. 110-111, 145-147] and [51].

3. For discussion of "administered" pricing, see [13], [22], [25], [26], and [41].

4. Evidence on the convexity of the Phillips curve with respect to the origin is presented, among other places, in [28, pp. 2-5], [33, p. 295], [40, pp. 191-193], and [41, p. 314].

5. This point is treated at greater length in [6, p. 349], [12, pp. 8-11], and [19, pp. 386-404].

6. Other writers have made the same comment about the original Gordon study. See [18, pp. 122, 161-165].

7. The results of our preliminary analyses using the original form of this variable are given [5].

8. The Phase II regulations regarding the maximum allowable wage increases are enumerated in detail in [14]. They are briefly summarized in [6, pp. 355-357].

9. See [1] and [9].

10. The transformations and assumptions made by Gordon in deriving a Phillips curve from the original DLA wage equation are described in [18, pp. 136-140, 149-153].

Chapter 3
An Imposed Lag Adjustment Model

1. See [12].

2. See [12, pp. 8-11] and [19, pp. 387, 390-394].

3. Evidence on the convexity of the relationship between unemployment and the rate of change in wages is presented, among other places, in [28, pp. 2-5], [33, p. 295], [40, pp. 191-193], and [41, p. 314].

4. See [12, p. 21].

5. For discussions of "administered" pricing, see [13], [22], [25], [26], and [41].

6. See [12, p. 28] and [18, p. 121].

7. See [1] and [9].

8. See [12, p. 35-36].

Chapter 4
A Current Period Adjustment Model

1. See [42].

2. See [42, p. 284].

3. Phillips' seminal discussion of hysteresis loops appears in [37]. For an amplified treatment of the subject, see [28, pp. 19-23].

4. For a discussion of the alternative interpretations that can be given to a Koyck lag, see [21, pp. 300-303, 316-317].

5. This point is explained in [21, pp. 303-320].

6. See [21, pp. 304-305].

7. See [24].

Chapter 5
A Comparison of the Three Models

1. See [6, p. 351], [18, pp. 159-164], and [19, pp. 400-406].

2. See the note to Table 2-3 in Chapter 2 and [46, pp. 33-38].

3. See [1] and [9].

Chapter 6
The Wage and Price Impacts of the Economic Stabilization Program

1. For a similar discussion of the same point, see [19, pp. 408-410].

2. Reasons for the wage and price impacts of the freeze and Phase II are discussed in [3], [6, p. 375], and [38, pp. 286-289].

3. See [35], [36], and [39, pp. 12-14].

4. See [32].

5. See [39, pp. 13-14].

Chapter 7
Implications of the Analysis

1. See, for example, [3], [7], [38], and [49, p. 76].

2. For analyses of such claims, see [32], [43], and [45].

3. See [3] and [6].

4. See [6, pp. 355-357, 361-367, 381-382].

5. See [2], [20], and [48, pp. 29-35].

Appendix B
Sources of Data

1. See [18, p. 153].
2. See [32, pp. 422, 440].
3. See [18, p. 155].
4. See [18, pp. 154-155].

References

[1] Aigner, Dennis J., "A Note on Verification of Computer Simulation Models," *Management Science,* Vol. 18, No. 11 (July, 1972), 615-619.

[2] "AFL-CIO Statement on Phase II Policy," *Washington Post* (March 23, 1972), A8. Reprinted as AFL-CIO Executive Council, *The Nixon Economic Program* (Washington, D.C.: American Federation of Labor and Congress of Industrial Organization, 1973).

[3] Askin, A. Bradley, "Inflation and Enforcement of Phase IV: Prospects and Proposals."

[4] _____ and Kraft, John, *Report on Econometric Wage and Price Models,* report prepared for the Division of Price Analysis, Office of Price Policy, Price Commission (November, 1972).

[5] _____ "Similarities and Differences among Three Alternative Models of the Inflation Process, with a Preliminary Evaluation of Phase II."

[6] Bosworth, Barry, "Phase II: The U.S. Experiment with an Incomes Policy," *Brookings Papers on Economic Activity,* No. 2, 1972, 343-383.

[7] _____ , "The Current Inflation: Malign Neglect?," *Brookings Papers on Economic Activity,* No. 1, 1973, 263-284.

[8] Chow, Gregory C., "Tests of Equality between Sets of Coefficients in Two Linear Regressions," *Econometrica,* Vol. 28, No. 3 (July, 1960), 591-605.

[9] Cohen, K.J. and Cyert, Richard M., "Computer Models in Dynamic Economics," *Quarterly Journal of Economics,* Vol. 75, No. 1 (February, 1961), 112-127.

[10] Dick-Mireaux, L.A., "The Interrelationship between Cost and Price Changes, 1946-1959," *Oxford Economic Papers,* New Series, Vol. 13, No. 3 (October, 1961), 267-292.

[11] Durbin, J., "Testing for Serial Correlation in Least-Squares Regression When Some of the Regressors Are Lagged Dependent Variables," *Econometrica,* Vol. 38, No. 3 (May, 1970), 410-421.

[12] Eckstein, Otto and Brinner, Roger, *The Inflation Process in the United States,* United States Joint Economic Committee of Congress, Ninety-second Congress, 2nd session (Washinton, D.C.: U.S. Government Printing Office, 1972).

[13] Eckstein, Otto and Fromm, Gary, "The Price Equation," *American Economic Review,* Vol. 48, No. 5 (December, 1968), 1159-1183.

[14] *Economic Stabilization,* Title 6, Code of Federal Regulations (Washington, D.C.: U.S. Government Printing Office, 1972).

[15] Fisher, Franklin M., "Tests of Equality between Sets of Coefficients in

Two Linear Regressions: An Expository Note," *Econometrica,* Vol. 38, No. 2 (March, 1970), 361-366.

[16] Fisher, Irving, "A Statistical Relation between Unemployment and Price Changes," reprinted in *Journal of Political Economy,* Vol. 81, No. 2, Part I (March-April, 1973), 496-502.

[17] Goldstein, Morris, "The Trade-Off between Inflation and Unemployment: A Survey of the Econometric Evidence for Selected Countries," *Staff Papers, International Monetary Fund,* Vol. 19, No. 3 (November, 1972), 647-698.

[18] Gordon, Robert J., "Inflation in Recession and Recovery," *Brookings Papers on Economic Activity,* No. 1, 1971, 105-166.

[19] ——— , "Wage-Price Controls and the Shifting Phillips Curve," *Brookings Papers on Economic Activity,* No. 2, 1972, 385-430.

[20] Heller, Walter W., "The Future of Wage-Price Controls," *Wall Street Journal,* Pacific Coast Edition (October 5, 1971), 12.

[21] Johnston, J., *Econometric Methods,* 2nd Edition (New York: McGraw-Hill Book Company, 1972).

[22] Kaplan, A.D.N., Dirlan, J.B., and Lanzillotti, Robert F., *Pricing in Big Business—A Case Approach* (Washington, D.C.: Brookings Institution, 1958).

[23] Kmenta, Jan, *Elements of Econometrics* (New York: The MacMillan Company, 1971).

[24] Kuh, E., "A Productivity Theory of Wage Levels—An Alternative to the Phillips Curve," *Review of Economic Studies,* Vol. 34, No. 100 (October, 1967), 333-360.

[25] Laden, Ben E., "Perfect Competition, Average Cost Pricing and the Price Equation," *Review of Economics and Statistics,* Vol. 54, No. 1 (February, 1972), 84-88.

[26] Lanzillotti, Robert F., "Pricing Objectives in Large Companies," *American Economic Review,* Vol. 48, No. 5 (December, 1958), 921-940.

[27] ——— and Roberts, Blaine, "An Assessment of the U.S. Experiment with an Incomes Policy," paper presented at the Tulane University Conference on Incomes Policies, April, 1973.

[28] Lipsey, Richard G., "The Relation between Unemployment and the Rate of Change of Money Wage Rates in the United Kingdom, 1862-1957: A Further Analysis," *Economica,* New Series, Vol. 27, No. 105 (February, 1960), 1-31.

[29] MacRae, C. Duncan, Schweitzer, Stuart O., and Holt, Charles C., "Job Search, Labor Turnover, and the Phillips Curve: An International Comparison," *1970 Proceedings of the Business and Economic Statistics Section,* American Statistical Association, 560-564.

[30] Moffat, William R., "Taxes in the Price Equation: Textiles and Rubber," *Review of Economics and Statistics,* Vol. 50, No. 3 (August, 1970), 253-261.

[31] Nerlove, M. and Wallis, K.F., "Use of the Durbin-Watson Statistic in Inappropriate Situations," *Econometrica,* Vol. 34, No. 1 (January, 1966), 235-238.

[32] Perry, George L., "Changing Labor Markets and Inflation," *Brookings Papers on Economic Activity,* No. 3, 1970, 411-441.

[33] _____ , "The Determinants of Wage Rate Changes and the Inflation-Unemployment Trade-Off for the United States," *Review of Economic Studies,* Vol. 31, No. 88 (October, 1964), 287-308.

[34] _____ , *Unemployment, Money Wage Rates, and Inflation* (Cambridge: The MIT Press, 1966).

[35] _____ , "Wages and the Guideposts," *American Economic Review,* Vol. 57, No. 4 (September, 1967), 897-904.

[36] _____ , Anderson, Paul S., Wachter, Michael L., and Throop, Adrian W., "Wages and the Guideposts: Comments and Reply," *American Economic Review,* Vol. 59, No. 3 (June, 1969), 351-370.

[37] Phillips, A.W., "The Relationship between Unemployment and the Rate of Change of Money Wage Rates in the United Kingdom, 1861-1957," *Economica,* New Series, Vol. 25, No. 100 (November, 1958), 283-299.

[38] Poole, William, "Wage-Price Controls: Where Do We Go from Here," *Brookings Papers on Economic Activity,* No. 1, 1973, 285-302.

[39] Rees, Albert, *Wage-Price Policy* (New York: General Learning Corporation, 1971).

[40] Samuelson, Paul A. and Solow, Robert M., "Analytical Aspects of Anti-Inflation Policy," *American Economic Review,* Vol. 50, No. 2 (May, 1960), 177-194.

[41] Schultze, Charles L. and Tryon, Joseph L., "Prices and Wages," in Dusenberry, James, Fromm, Gary, Klein, L.R., and Kuh, Edwin (eds.), *Brookings Quarterly Econometric Model of the U.S. Economy* (Chicago: Rand-McNally and Company, 1965), 281-333.

[42] Siebert, Calvin D. and Zaidi, Mahmood A., "The Short-Run Wage-Price Mechanism in U.S. Manufacturing," *Western Economic Journal,* Vol. 9, No. 3 (September, 1971), 278-288.

[43] Simler, N.J. and Tella, A., "Labor Reserves and the Phillips Curve," *Review of Economics and Statistics,* Vol. 50, No. 1 (February, 1968), 32-49.

[44] Spencer, Roger W., "The National Plans to Curb Unemployment and Inflation," *Federal Reserve Bank of St. Louis Review,* Vol. 55, No. 4 (April, 1973), 2-13.

[45] Tella, Alfred, "Was Employment Rise in June Real or Imaginary," *Washington Post* (July 16, 1972), E1, E8.

[46] Theil, Henri, *Economic Forecasts and Policy* (Amsterdam: North-Holland Publishing Company, 1965).

[47] Turnovsky, Stephen J., "The Expectations Hypothesis and the Aggregate Wage Equation: Some Empirical Evidence for Canada," *Economica,* New Series, Vol. 38, No. 149 (February, 1972), 1-17.

[48] United States Joint Economic Committee of Congress, *Report on the January 1973 Economic Report of the President,* Ninety-third Congress, 1st session (Washington, D.C.: U.S. Government Printing Office, 1973).

[49] United States Senate Committee on Banking, Housing and Urban Affairs, *Hearings on Economic Stabilization Legislation,* Ninety-third Congress, 1st session (Washington, D.C.: U.S. Government Printing Office, 1972).

[50] Vroman, Wayne, "Manufacturing Wage Behavior with Special Reference to the Period 1962-1966," *Review of Economics and Statistics,* Vol. 52, No. 2 (May, 1970), 160-167.

[51] Yohe, William P., and Karnosky, Denis S., "Interest Rates and Price Level Changes, 1952-69," *Federal Reserve Bank of St. Louis Review,* Vol. 51, No. 12 (December, 1969), 18-38.

About the Authors

A. Bradley Askin is an assistant professor in the Graduate School of Administration at the University of California, Irvine. He is also associated with the Rand Corporation. He received the Ph.D. in economics from the Massachusetts Institute of Technology in 1970.

John Kraft is an assistant professor in the economics department at the University of Florida. Currently he is employed by the Department of Housing and Urban Development as a Brookings Institution Economic Policy Fellow. He received the Ph.D. in economics from the University of Pittsburgh in 1971.